All About Pruning

Created and designed by
the editorial staff of
ORTHO BOOKS

Project Editor
Susan A. Roth

Writers
Fred K. Buscher
Susan A. McClure

Illustrator
Ron Hildebrand

Photographer
Douglas Ross

Designer
Gary Hespenheide

Ortho Books

Editorial Director
Christine Robertson

Production Director
Ernie S. Tasaki

Managing Editors
Michael D. Smith
Sally W. Smith

System Manager
Katherine Parker

National Sales Manager
Charles H. Aydelotte

Marketing Specialist
Dennis M. Castle

Operations Assistant
Georgiann Wright

Distribution Specialist
Barbara F. Steadham

Senior Technical Analyst
J. A. Crozier, Jr., PhD.

Acknowledgments

Copy Chief
Melinda E. Levine

Copyeditor
Susan Lang

Layout Editor
Linda M. Bouchard

Editorial Coordinator
Cass Dempsey

Proofreader
Frances Bowles

Indexer
Frances Bowles

Editorial Assistants
Karen K. Johnson
Tamara Mallory

System Coordinator
Laurie Prather

Administrative Assistant
Cindy Ellis

Art Director
Craig Bergquist

Production by
Lezlly Freier

Separations by
Color Tech Corp.

Lithographed by
Webcrafters, Inc.

Address all inquiries to
Ortho Books
Chevron Chemical Company
Consumer Products Division
Box 5047
San Ramon, CA 94583

Copyright © 1978, 1989
Chevron Chemical Company
All rights reserved under international and Pan-American copyright conventions.

2 3 4 5 6 7 8 9
90 91 92 93 94

ISBN 0-89721-198-7
Library of Congress Catalog Card
Number 88-63844

Chevron Chemical Company
6001 Bollinger Canyon Road, San Ramon, CA 94583

Consultants
David Barnett, PhD.
  Planting Fields Arboretum
  Oyster Bay, N.Y.
David C. Ferree, PhD.
  Ohio State University
  Wooster, Ohio

Photographers
Names of photographers are followed by the page numbers on which their work appears. R = right, C = center, L = left, T = top, B = bottom.

William Aplin/Ortho Slide Library: 35BL, 77L
Liz Ball/Garden Portraits: 40M, 59L
Laurie Black/Ortho Slide Library: 71R
John Blaustein/Ortho Slide Library: title page
Karen Bussolini: 6T, 6B, 32, 35R
Josephine Coatsworth/Ortho Slide Library: 98
Derek Fell: 4, 7, 8R, 57R, 60L, 62, 93
David Goldberg: 18
Harry Haralambou: 37R, 45M, 58TR, 73, 95L
Saxon Holt: 45T, 58BR, 78L, 87R
Saxon Holt/Ortho Slide Library: 57BL, 78L, 81L, 81R, 83TL
Susan A. McClure: 20, 88
Michael Landis/Ortho Slide Library: 10BR, 40L, 51, 55BL, 79L, 81TR, 103
Michael McKinley/Ortho Slide Library: 34L, 37TL, 54L, 55TL, 64T, 64B, 76L, 77R, 81M, 83BL, 85L, 85R, 87L
James K. McNair/Ortho Slide Library: 10TL, 59R
Maggie Oster: 36L, 38R, 39BR, 61R, 78R, 83R
Pamela Peirce: 27, 76R
Pamela Peirce/Ortho Slide Library: 41R, 61L, 81BR, 82L, 82TR, 84L, 87TL
Douglas Ross: 8L, 14, 15L, 15R, 23R, 29TL, 29TR, 29BL, 33T, 33M, 33B, 47TL, 47TR, 47BL, 47BR, 56R, 65L, 66L, 66R, 68, 72L, 72R
Susan A. Roth: 10TR, 28, 34R, 42, 44, 50B, 54R, 55R, 71L, 79R, 81L, 82BR, 95R, 97, 108
Susan A. Roth/Ortho Slide Library: 23L, 34R, 36R, 39L, 41L, 45B, 50T, 84R, 85R, 102
Anita Sabarese: 36M, 57TL, 85L
Ortho Slide Library: 35TR, 37BR, 38L, 39TR, 40R, 56L, 90, 99

Special thanks to
Eileen Barnett, Oyster Bay, N.Y.
Jake Barnett, Oyster Bay, N.Y.
Richard and Diana Debree, Stony Brook, N.Y.
John R. Marchetto, Northport, N.Y.
Hermin P. Michaels, Jr., Huntington Station, N.Y.
Ellen Pearce, Gardeners Extraordinaire,
  San Francisco, Calif.
Planting Fields Arboretum, Oyster Bay, N.Y.
Mark Schneider, Stony Brook, N.Y.
Emily Thomas and Bryce Hoole, Stony Brook, N.Y.
Brookside Gardens, Kensington, Calif. (photo site 58BR)

Front Cover
For best healing, a tree branch should be cut carefully so as to leave the branch collar intact.

Title Page
A pruning saw is the tool of choice for cutting through small branches larger than 2 inches in diameter.

Back Cover
Top left: Lopping shears cut well through the tough canes of a rosebush.
Bottom left: When removing a rose for indoor display, cut just above an outward-facing bud.
Top right: A pole pruner makes it easy to saw off overhead branches.
Bottom right: A small, curved pruning saw is easy to manipulate in tight spaces, such as between these forsythia trunks.

All About Pruning

Pruning Techniques

Learn to be an expert pruner by understanding where, when, and why to prune. This chapter explains everything you need to know to keep your plants in shape and to select the proper tools for every pruning job.

Correct pruning is part science, part art. The science comes into play when you begin to understand how plants grow and respond to different pruning cuts. Understanding this response helps the gardener develop a good sense about how, where, and when to make a pruning cut. The art comes into play as you shape a plant—deciding which branches to remove and which to leave intact, which to shorten, and which to allow to grow. The result is a tree or shrub that grows into the shape envisioned in the mind's eye—a shape that suits the plant and looks appropriate in the garden setting.

In the same way that the artistic side of pruning changes as tastes and preferred landscape styles change, so does the scientific side of pruning evolve with new discoveries. Pruning techniques employed today are different from—and better than—those used 10 years ago because of recent discoveries about how woody plants respond to pruning wounds. And these important changes in technique mean healthier, longer-lived trees and shrubs. Improper pruning can actually harm valuable trees.

The trees and shrubs in this naturalistic garden are carefully pruned to maintain their pleasing shape and prevent them from crowding the path.

WHY PRUNE?

Pruning is essential in preserving the integrity and scale of the landscape design. Although this is the primary motive of most homeowners who prune their trees and shrubs, there are other equally important reasons to prune. Regular and correct pruning keeps shrubs and trees healthy and vigorous and prevents potential problems. Properly pruned fruit trees will bear larger crops and ward off diseases better. Carefully pruned flowering shrubs not only blossom profusely year after year, but also remain a desirable size. When a tree is grown in a home landscape rather than in a natural woodland, pruning can guide its branch structure so that when it's mature, the branches are strong and resist storm damage.

Controlling Size

It is often difficult to imagine just how large a newly planted shrub will become over the years; homeowners commonly plant trees and shrubs too close to each other, too near the house, or in a location where their ultimate size is unacceptable. Once planted, a shrub may be left to its own devices until it is seriously crowding other plants or blocking a view. A tree may be left to develop branches that poke the side of the house or rest on the roof. Pruning and training early on will prevent the need for major pruning later.

Many homeowners face the problem of foundation shrubs growing so tall that they obscure windows, blocking light and air. Foundation plantings were originally conceived at the turn of the century to hide exposed foundation walls. At that time, basements were shallowly dug and foundation walls had to rise well above ground to allow enough room for a coal-fired furnace. Planting shrubs around the base of a house was the logical way to hide the basement walls.

Today foundation plantings are common even though basements are deeper and foundations no longer require as much concealing. Among the most common foundation plants are evergreens such as yew, juniper, arborvitae, and false cypress, which mature at heights of 6 to 10 feet or more. It is little wonder that these tall-growing foundation plants soon obscure the first-floor windows. Many houses become dwarfed by the overgrown shrubs surrounding

Top: Low-growing shrubs, which require only minimal pruning, are ideal for landscaping a contemporary house that has low, easy-to-conceal foundation walls. Bottom: Pruning transformed this overgrown viburnum, which was obscuring the garage window, into a small, slender-trunked tree. A porthole—to allow a view through the window—was crafted without disfiguring the plant.

them. Annual pruning can control most foundation shrubs and can keep their size within the proper limits.

When trees and shrubs are pruned at planting time and given yearly attention, they can be kept at a desirable size. If they are allowed to grow too large, drastic pruning methods must be employed to dramatically reduce them. However, when done properly rejuvenation needn't spoil a shrub's appearance.

Choosing a Natural or Formal Style

The pruning techniques chosen determine whether the pruned plant takes on a formal shape or retains its natural shape. For a naturalistic effect, pruning should be inspired by the plant's normal growth habit. Pruned naturalistically a shrub or tree maintains its usual habit and growth rate; only a little attention is required each year to maintain the desired size and shape. See pages 10 and 11 for more information on naturalistic pruning methods.

In some landscape designs, formal shapes and neatly defined edges look elegant. Formal landscape designs use square and round shapes and sharply drawn lines for both structures and plants. The natural form of the plant is changed and pruned into the geometrical shape

Pruning History

Wherever and whenever people grow plants they also prune them. Pruning is, in fact, an ancient skill. It is essential to the art of bonsai, introduced from China into Japan in the 13th and 14th centuries and still practiced today. The bonsai artist attempts to create a picturesquely twisted and dwarfed tree reminiscent of those trees found growing in harsh mountain conditions. The artist simulates the effects of frozen, rocky soil and biting winds, which can dwarf normally towering trees, by severely pruning the bonsai's roots and shoots. These trees are then confined in shallow bonsai pots for decades, even centuries, further stunting their growth. Further pruning of new growth to emphasize the line of the trunk and create clouds of foliage develops the shape and feeling that epitomizes the essence of the art of bonsai.

Grape pruning is mentioned in both the Old and New Testaments. The earliest gardening volumes gave directions for pruning tree and bush fruits. Some of these ancient ideas, founded on a lifetime of observation, are still useful, but others have been outdated by modern technology and research or are not practical for a contemporary home gardener.

The ancient Greeks and Romans pruned potted plants into formal topiaries, which they used for decorating patios and the interiors of their homes. This practice eventually spread throughout the Roman Empire and resulted in formal parterre gardens like those at Versailles.

The Renaissance revival of classical order and design in art, literature, and architecture brought the importance of pruning to an all-time high in European gardens. Geometrical gardens, popular in the 14th through the 16th centuries, often were designed by architects. Rectangles, squares, and circles—forms used in architecture—were carried into the garden and into the plant shapes. The attempt to control the environment has seldom been stronger than during this Renaissance fascination with pruning plants into unnatural forms.

The earliest formal gardens in America, including those of George Washington and Thomas Jefferson, copied prevailing styles in England and Europe. They were the predecessors of a naturalistic and picturesque style of garden design and development, which began in the late 18th century. As Americans grew more settled and secure in their own unique traditions

The formal garden of the Governor's Palace in Colonial Williamsburg, Virginia, is typical of European garden design of that time.

by the mid to late 19th century, naturalistic gardens became the vogue.

Contemporary garden design draws from all these sectors of history. Today's gardens can be formal or informal in flavor, depending upon the desire of the homeowner. No one pruning style is appropriate for all plants or garden designs. The pruning techniques described here will provide alternative methods for creating the landscape setting suited to home and gardening needs.

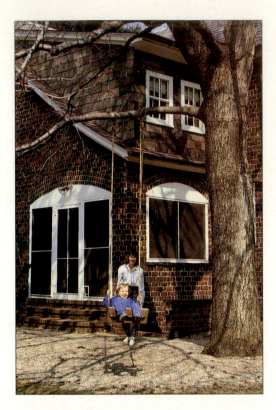

Left: A sturdy branch at a right angle to the tree trunk offers the perfect place to hang a swing.
Right: When scaffold branches are spaced radially around the tree, they allow for easy climbing by young adventurers.

that reinforces the design. Since the natural shape and size of the plant are changed by pruning, the type of plant becomes less important. A plant that responds well to formal clipping is usually selected; boxwood and yew are the most popular choices.

Different pruning techniques make a hedge either a formal, uniform green wall or an informal row of closely planted shrubs with softer edges. The sheared hedge, an important element of classical European gardens, demands frequent pruning to maintain its tidy formality. A formal hedge should be pruned two or more times each year, depending on the plants' rate of growth. Informally pruned hedges, on the other hand, may only need pruning once a year to keep them looking good and within bounds (see pages 50 to 53 for hedge-pruning techniques).

Increasing Vigor

Regular pruning of shrubs by a technique called gradual renewal pruning can keep a landscape young, vigorous and healthy. Yearly pruning encourages old growth to give way to new wood, which flowers more profusely and is more resistant to disease and insects. Even neglected and overgrown shrubs can be renewed gradually by removing the oldest and tallest branches over several years.

Removing branches also allows the sun to penetrate deep into the interior of the plant. When exposed to sun, foliage expands to its fullest, maximizing photosynthesis—the process whereby plants produce food energy to power their growth. Regular pruning spreads the regrowth and rejuvenation effect throughout the entire plant.

Directing Growth

Often newly purchased shade trees bear undesirable and structurally unsound branches that are best removed after planting. Some nurseries encourage side branch growth by cutting back young shade trees to a height of 5 or 6 feet. Although these young trees appear compact and well-proportioned—that's why they are pruned to this shape—the flourish of lateral and upright branches may be too low to the ground, too close together, or lacking a central trunk. Right after planting is the ideal time to begin developing a better arrangement of branches with minimal pruning.

A tree or shrub can be pruned to fulfill a particular function. Often trees can be trained while young to develop branches that are suitable for climbing or holding a swing. To create a tree for children to climb, begin with a young specimen with a horizontal or wide-spreading habit—for example, apple, crab apple, or pin oak—and prune selectively to promote low branches that spiral radially upward. An appropriate tree for a swing is one with a strong, completely horizontal branch 10 to 20 feet aboveground that has no nearby branches to interfere with the swing's ropes.

Small-leaved trees, such as thornless honey locust, yellowwood, dogwood, zelkova, or katsura, naturally allow filtered sun to penetrate to plants below. Light levels can be further increased by pruning away lower limbs. Plant trees such as these in a grove to create the low-light setting needed for a shade garden. It is just as easy to create a shade garden beneath more densely foliaged trees—under whose thick canopies grasses and other plants can't naturally grow—by removing some branches to allow more light to filter to the ground. The trees may need yearly thinning to maintain the desirable light level (see pages 30 and 31 for pruning techniques to use for mature trees).

Protecting Your Investment

Mature trees make a property more valuable; realtors know that homes with well-kept lawns, large trees, and pleasing ornamental plants sell more quickly and for more money than those not as well landscaped. A Michigan State University Forestry study concluded that healthy trees can add as much as 15 percent to the value of a half-acre residence. Pruning, which preserves the integrity of a landscape and the health and vigor of plants, is an important way to protect the investment. Each year, as the plants increase in size, the investment in time and care grows. A mature shade tree, which may take 25 years to begin to approach full size and spread, is practically irreplaceable; it could cost several to many thousands of dollars to replace it with a tree of equal size.

On the other hand, neglected trees with dead branches, cavities, or poor shapes can be a liability. Since removing unhealthy trees is costly, taking proper care of plants and pruning them when necessary can reap a financial reward as well as beautify the property.

The dense canopy of a mature shade tree may prevent sun from reaching the ground; this is particularly disastrous for lawn grasses, most varieties of which suffer in more than 65 percent shade. Excessive shade reduces the vigor of grass and makes it fall prey to powdery mildew fungus; eventually it will die. Solve this problem by pruning tree branches or by underplanting the tree with shade-tolerant plants rather than a lawn. Removing some branches permits additional sunlight to filter through to the plants below. On young trees removing a few low-hanging branches is often adequate. However, large shade trees may need repeated thinning for a dense stand of turf to survive or even shade-tolerant ground covers to thrive.

Repairing Storm Damage

Snowstorms, hurricanes, tornadoes, and thunderstorms can damage even properly pruned trees. Of course, trees that have weak limbs or a poor branching structure are more susceptible to storm damage than ones trained to have sturdy branches and a more open canopy. When severe weather causes tree limbs to snap, the damage can often be repaired and the tree saved with the proper pruning techniques. The techniques are similar to those used for removing large healthy branches (see page 29).

When severe winds break or damage branches high in a tree, there is little recourse other than to seek professional tree-care help. These branches are often hazardous to remove and may require roping to lower them safely to the ground.

After pruning a severely damaged tree, increase its vigor by giving the tree extra care. Consider irrigating, supporting the tree with guy wires, fertilizing, mulching, and controlling pests to help the tree recover.

PRUNING STYLES

Home landscapes have a sameness about them that originated around the turn of the century. At that time, homeowners began to surround the perimeters of their houses with shrubbery to hide high, unattractive foundations. The shrubs were pruned into neat, geometrical shapes inspired by Renaissance gardens. This style of planting—and pruning—is all too often repeated today, even though modern homes don't have high, exposed foundations. Many innovative landscape designers are instead creating gardens and groups of shrubs around a house, rather than a row of traditional foundation plants.

Formal and Informal Styles

Formal gardens appear neat, well-ordered, and under the complete control of the gardener. Long, elegant hedges define garden spaces and mark boundaries. Plant shapes are geometrical and shrubs are usually sheared (see page 13) into individual balls, cones, or boxes. This traditional style enhances some garden settings, in which formality and an elegant look are required.

Today garden styles tend to be more informal, with an emphasis on a naturalistic look. Gardeners and horticulturists appreciate the natural shapes of plants; many garden designers emphasize plants in groups or masses reflecting naturalistic, free-form styles. In an informal setting, shrubs are not pruned into rigid shapes but are thinned (see page 13) as needed to emphasize their layers of tiered branches, gracefully cascading limbs, or irregular outlines.

Pruning Controversy

Confusion often arises among homeowners and even some horticulturists about the appropriate way to prune. The controversy centers around the choice between formal and informal pruning techniques. People imitate what they see, assuming that it is correct—and what they see most often are plants indiscriminately sheared into rigid, formal shapes

at the expense of the natural beauty of the plants. The unique blending of natural forms, textures, colors, and sizes is what produces an aesthetically pleasing landscape. Well-pruned shrubbery that follows the natural lines of plants can still be neat and controlled while creating a softer, more informal setting. Many commercial landscape maintenance contractors who realize this still have a difficult time convincing their customers that the natural shape is a desirable alternative.

Top left: Tidy shearing and symmetrical shrub placement create a formal effect. Top right: When pruned by thinning, azaleas retain their graceful shape. Bottom: When pruned by shearing, the shape becomes geometrical.

A survey of shrubs in the front yards of most neighborhoods would likely reveal the predominance of uniform balls, boxes, and cones. Yet few landscapes actually look best arranged as a series of geometrical shapes. Many of the shrubs treated this way not only would look more attractive, but also would grow and flower better if shaped naturally. Inappropriate pruning can ruin a plant's natural beauty, while appropriate pruning can enhance it. Boxwood and privet can be pruned into rectangular hedges that act as a garden boundary. Plants used to denote boundaries can look impressive when sheared formally; the same plants look forbidding and stiff when sheared into a boxy foundation hedge. Most of the grace and beauty of a flowering shrub like forsythia is lost when it is pruned into a rigid shape; the flowers are jammed together into a mass of color. The plant looks better when the branches arch and cascade toward the ground, displaying the flowers on a more open structure.

Just because some neighbors prune their shrubs into rigid outlines should not dictate the pruning style for the neighborhood—this book offers alternate techniques and styles. Careful observation will reveal where formality is appropriate and where informality is better suited. It is best to choose the style that matches the house and garden setting, rather than copy inappropriate pruning.

UNDERSTANDING PRUNING AND PLANT GROWTH

Some fundamental knowledge about how plants grow explains a great deal about the way they respond to pruning cuts. By understanding the basics of plant growth a gardener is able to prune more intuitively.

The Role of the Bud

Almost all new growth on trees and shrubs develops from buds on the branches. There are three types of buds: dormant, latent, and adventitious. Dormant buds form during one growing season and remain dormant until the next growth period when, depending upon the type of bud, they grow into stems, leaves, or flowers. New stems arise first from dormant buds at the branch tip (called terminal buds). Side branches develop from the dormant buds

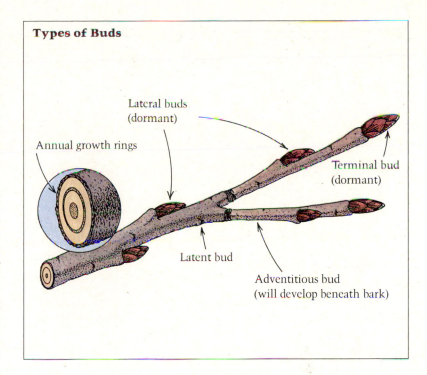

Types of Buds

Annual growth rings

Lateral buds (dormant)

Terminal bud (dormant)

Latent bud

Adventitious bud (will develop beneath bark)

on the side of a branch (called lateral buds). When lateral buds are located at the base of a leaf, they are called axillary buds. Some axillary buds produce leaves or flowers.

Not every bud actually grows into a branch, leaf, or flower. Some buds on young twigs remain inactive for many seasons. When dormant buds persist on older stems, they are known as latent buds; they remain at or near the surface of the bark as the branch gets larger. Both dormant buds and latent buds are strongly linked to the stem's pipeline of water and nutrients by a connection called a bud trace. These latent buds are the plant's insurance. Should a branch be cut or broken above a dormant or latent bud, a new shoot can quickly grow from the bud.

Adventitious buds develop where no buds previously existed. These sometimes grow after a branch is wounded or cut back to mature tissue. These buds differ from latent buds because they develop close to the branch surface from deeper mature tissue and are not connected by a bud trace; consequently, the branches that develop from adventitious buds are not strongly connected to the trunk or main branches and can be easily broken during a storm.

Improper pruning techniques, such as cutting branches back to stubs, often activate dormant or latent buds or cause adventitious buds to form behind the stub. For a number of

Response to Shearing a Shrub

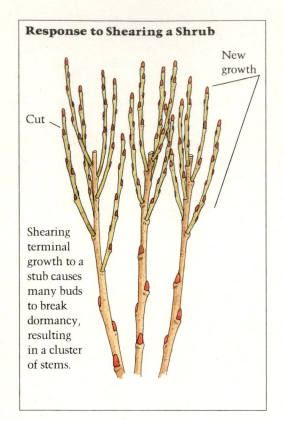

New growth

Cut

Shearing terminal growth to a stub causes many buds to break dormancy, resulting in a cluster of stems.

Response to Thinning a Shrub

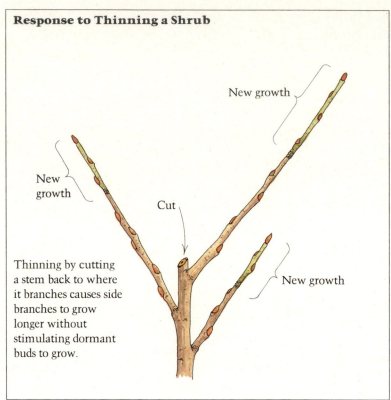

New growth

New growth

Cut

New growth

Thinning by cutting a stem back to where it branches causes side branches to grow longer without stimulating dormant buds to grow.

years, the young shoots that arise from these buds are weakly attached to the parent stems and are easily broken. Not until new layers of wood form annual growth rings around the branches are they strongly anchored.

Apical Dominance

By observing the current season's growth of a woody plant, you can see that few, if any, lateral buds close to the tip of the branch have grown into side branches. Not until a lateral bud is a long enough distance from the terminal bud—usually as a result of two or three seasons of growth—does it begin to grow. This phenomenon, called apical dominance, is controlled by a hormone in the terminal bud that is known as auxin. This hormone suppresses the growth of the other buds, signaling them to remain dormant. Buds farther and farther away receive weaker and weaker signals, until they are released from dormancy and begin to grow.

This hormonal effect determines a plant's branching pattern and its response to pruning. As long as the terminal bud remains alive, it will be the first to grow in the spring. This natural system results in an orderly, controlled growth rate and gives a characteristic shape to all species of plants—but prune off

the terminal bud and growth patterns become drastically altered.

The science of pruning lies in understanding and manipulating bud growth. Removing a terminal bud releases dormant, latent, or adventitious buds from the growth inhibition caused by apical dominance. Removing the terminal bud alters the orderly, natural growth patterns. Many of the buds behind the cut sprout into branches; where one stem once grew, now a cluster of many stems emerges. This growth pattern is nowhere more apparent than on a sheared hedge or a tree cut flat below an electric utility line. Not only does the plant lose its natural shape, but exceptionally fast growth creates a branch structure that resembles a candelabra. On the other hand, the growth pattern of a plant is preserved by pruning back a stem or side branch to where buds have already broken dormancy and formed a side shoot. The terminal bud on the lateral branch may then assume apical dominance.

PRUNING CUTS

Different pruning cuts result in different growth patterns. There are several types of pruning cuts, determined by where they are made on the stem in relation to dormant buds and side branches.

Thinning

The thinning cut involves cutting off a shrub or tree branch at its point of origin on the parent branch. Thinning cuts may also be used to shorten a branch by cutting it back to a crotch (where the branch forms a Y). The terminal bud of the remaining branch assumes apical dominance and prevents other dormant buds from breaking dormancy and growing into branches. Thinning the major branches of a tree is called drop crotching; this technique dramatically reduces the size of a tree while maintaining its natural shape (see page 30).

Pruning a shrub by using thinning cuts reduces its size without stimulating much unnecessary new growth. That's why horticulture departments in major universities recommend thinning as the best pruning method for most shrubs and trees. Thinning controls size and rejuvenates the plant, making it more vigorous, healthier, and stronger.

Heading

When a branch is headed it is cut to a stub, lateral bud, or a small-diameter lateral branch. The cut is called stubbing if a large branch is headed leaving a stub. Since heading removes the terminal bud, apical dominance is lost and many vigorous new shoots develop from buds directly below the cut; buds lower on the branch remain inhibited. Fruit trees, which produce few side branches, may be headed to encourage branching.

Sometimes street trees are headed under utility wires to remove interfering branches. Not only does the resultant flush of growth soon become a problem, but the tree also loses the beauty and dignity of its natural shape.

Shearing

Shearing, similar in principle to heading, is a pruning cut that removes short lengths of top growth. The cut may fall above or below a bud, often leaving a stub. Because shearing removes the terminal buds on all the stem tips, a flush of new growth directly behind the cuts results in a dense canopy of exterior foliage. The shearing cut is best reserved for hedges or topiaries in formal gardens. Some shrubs adapt better to being sheared than others; many otherwise beautiful plants can be ruined by inappropriate shearing.

Heading a Tree

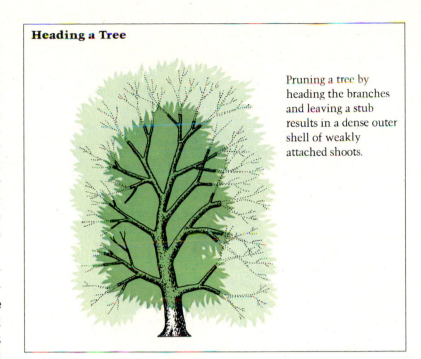

Pruning a tree by heading the branches and leaving a stub results in a dense outer shell of weakly attached shoots.

Thinning a Tree

Pruning a tree by thinning branches back to side branches and leaving no stubs produces a more open and stronger branching pattern.

Pinching

Pinching off the tip of a succulent stem produces a growth response similar to heading cuts made on woody stems. Pinching young annual and perennial flowering plants encourages bushy growth behind the pinch. Likewise, branching of the leaders (the terminal shoots) of young trees can be induced by pinching off 1 to 2 inches of new growth. The resultant new growth must be thinned as the branches begin to grow or else these branches will compete with the main leader.

CHOOSING A PRUNING CUT

In most cases trees and shrubs that need pruning—for whatever reason—should be thinned. This results in the most natural appearance and in strong growth that is more resistant to storm damage. Plants that are thinned grow at a healthy pace, but remain neater and require less frequent pruning than plants that are headed or sheared. Shearing creates more individual stems, which each produce terminal growth; this, in turn, stimulates more new growth. Thinning removes terminal growth, thus slowing the amount of new growth.

Pruning for a Natural Shape

First observe the branching habit of the plant. If the plant has been sheared or improperly pruned, find a specimen that has retained its natural shape.

If a shrub forms layers of horizontal branches, try to encourage this type of shape, pruning back the higher branches more than those below to create a tiered effect. For a fountain-shaped shrub of cascading branches, thin overly long or gangly limbs.

In nature plants gradually self-prune by shedding dead branches at the point of attachment to another branch or trunk. Learn from this example: Prune back to the point of attachment, always leaving a terminal bud on the remaining branch to direct a natural growth pattern.

These natural forms lend themselves to planting in groups and masses, more suitable for most home landscapes than individual sheared cones, drums, balls, and squares.

Where a more formal appearance is desired, it is acceptable to shear shrubs. Keep in mind, however, that shearing actually overstimulates growth from the cut ends of the branches and means more work for the gardener in the long run.

WOUND HEALING

Research carried out over many years by the United States Forest Service has demonstrated that many old pruning ideas and practices are no longer valid. Botanists now know that healthy trees have the intrinsic ability to resist invasion of wood-decaying organisms. Trees can close off pockets of decay and prevent its spread into neighboring wood by a process called compartmentalization.

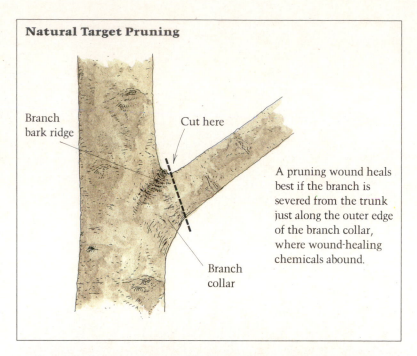

Natural Target Pruning

Branch bark ridge

Cut here

Branch collar

A pruning wound heals best if the branch is severed from the trunk just along the outer edge of the branch collar, where wound-healing chemicals abound.

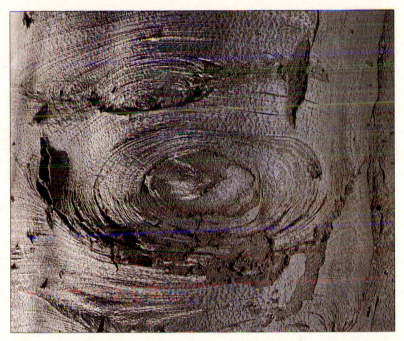

Opposite: Wounds heal best when the branch is sawed off just to the edge of the branch bark ridge, visible here in the crotch of the branch.

Left: One year after a branch of this beech tree was correctly removed at the branch bark ridge, healing callus has begun to form along the edges of the wound.

Right: Several years after a branch was properly removed, callus has completely covered the wound and the expanding trunk has all but engulfed the callus on the trunk where the branch once grew.

The structure of the branch connection to the trunk plays an important role in decay resistance. A swollen branch collar is usually visible at the point where a side branch connects to the woody parent stem or trunk. This collar results from the meeting of two patterns of growth: the branch and the trunk. The side branch probably developed from a lateral bud in its second season. As the season progressed, the annual growth ring of bark on the parent stem or trunk began to expand and surround the base of the new shoot. This phenomenon resembles a mechanical ball-and-socket connection. With each passing year the branch collar continues to grow around the base of the branch, strengthening the attachment. As the collar grows, it may compress the bark causing a visible ridge, called the branch bark ridge, to form where the branch tissue and the trunk tissue meet.

For woody plants the branch collar has special significance. It is a storehouse for chemicals known as phenolic compounds that are highly toxic to fungi. Research has shown that phenols help prevent decay-causing organisms from moving from injured or dying branches into healthy tissue.

If a branch is cut off flush with the parent branch or trunk—and the collar is removed as was once advised—the tree loses its natural protective barrier and decay organisms can more readily enter the wound. The latest advice employs a pruning method called *natural target pruning.* The branch is severed from the trunk at the edge of the branch collar where the concentration of phenolic compounds is high. A wound at the edge of the collar heals fastest and is most effective in repelling decay organisms. (See illustration on opposite page.)

Trees are able to shed dead branches, closing over their wounds with callus tissue to help prevent decay. Callus also forms over the surface of wood exposed by a pruning cut. Cuts made on the outside edge of the collar appear initially as a circle and later, when callus forms, as a doughnut. Each subsequent year the hole in the doughnut grows smaller until the wound is completely closed. An improper flush cut not only leaves an oval wound or larger area for callus to close but also removes the protective branch collar.

The speed of the healing process depends upon the health and vigor of the individual tree or shrub, as well as the quantity of food reserves in the plant. Trees that are long-lived are better able to compartmentalize, resist decay, and quickly close injuries than are weaker, short-lived species.

PRUNING TOOLS

Although the only pruning tool many homeowners possess is a pair of hedge shears, several other tools make pruning easy and are more appropriate for trimming plants. Hedge shears are designed to trim the stems of

Pruning Tools

Handheld pruning shears: Use for cutting stems up to ½" in diameter. Scissor types (illustrated) cut closer than anvil types, which can crush bark if not very sharp.

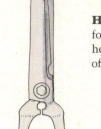

Hedge shears: Use for trimming formal hedges when a neat wall of foliage is the goal.

Wide-blade saw: Use this sturdy saw on the largest limbs. Its angled teeth work on the pull stroke—the opposite of how a carpenter's saw works.

Lopping shears: Their long handles provide extra leverage, making lopping shears capable of cutting through stems up to 1½" in diameter. Blades may be either anvil or scissor type.

Narrow curved pruning saw: The narrow curved blade makes this tool useful for sawing off crowded stems or branches with narrow angles of attachment.

Double-edged saw: One side of the blade has teeth that cut when the saw is pushed, making it useful for small branches; the other side has coarse teeth that cut both on the push and pull strokes, and is useful for removing larger branches.

Electric hedge shears: These electric-powered shears make quick work of major hedge-trimming jobs. They are faster and easier to use than manual shears, but must be used with care.

Bow saw: Bow saws are light in weight but strong enough to cut through large branches. The blades can be replaced.

Extension-pole loppers: These lopping shears mounted on the end of an extension pole are handy for clipping small overhead branches.

Extension-pole saw: Mounted on a long extendable pole, this saw is useful for removing small overhead or hard-to-reach tree branches.

Chain saw: Time- and labor-saving, chain saws make quick work of sawing through branches larger than 3" in diameter. They should be operated with extreme caution.

plants into flat wall-like surfaces on the top and sides of a hedge, as the name of the tool implies. These two-handed shears are designed for pruning hedges and for that purpose they are excellent—but don't use them for most pruning chores. Handheld pruning shears, long-handled lopping shears, and pruning saws are all suitable tools for pruning deciduous and evergreen shrubs, especially those in borders, foundations, and specimen plantings.

With hedge shears anyone, regardless of skill, can quickly prune a shrub into a rigid wall or ball. Using hand pruners to reveal the graceful shape of a plant takes a little time and more knowledge and skill, but is certainly within the ability of home gardeners. The first tool to buy is a pair of handheld pruning shears. Use these for cutting stems less than ½ inch thick. Choose from scissor types with sharpened blades that overlap or anvil-style pruners with a sharpened blade that cuts against a metal anvil. Scissor pruners are preferred by most professionals because they make closer, cleaner cuts than do anvil pruners. You need only sharpen one side of the beveled blade with a whetstone. Although anvil pruners are lightweight and less expensive, they tend to crush bark against the anvil if the blade is not kept sharp.

Better-quality shears have steel blades that keep a sharp edge longer and are more comfortable to use than are cheaper choices. Spending a little extra on a good pair is well worthwhile.

Lopping shears are long-handled pruners that provide extra leverage for cutting stouter branches. Use them to cut stems between ½ and 1½ inches in diameter. Using them for larger tasks may force the blades out of alignment. Loppers are especially handy for removing branches at the base of deciduous shrubs and thinning young branches on trees. Loppers are available in both scissor and anvil styles.

Use a pruning saw for cutting branches too large for hand pruners and loppers. Smaller, curved, narrow-bladed saws are useful in confined spaces. Choose a bow saw where there is more room. Unlike carpentry saws, pruning saws cut on the pull stroke; some have teeth on both sides, one edge coarse, the other fine. If cutting with a double-edged saw, be sure the teeth on the backside don't tear unintentionally into the bark on another branch.

How to Hold Handheld Pruning Shears

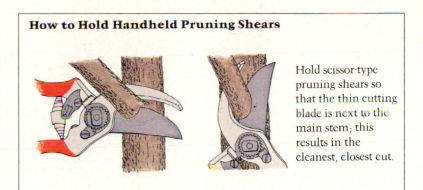

Hold scissor-type pruning shears so that the thin cutting blade is next to the main stem; this results in the cleanest, closest cut.

Where to Make Cuts

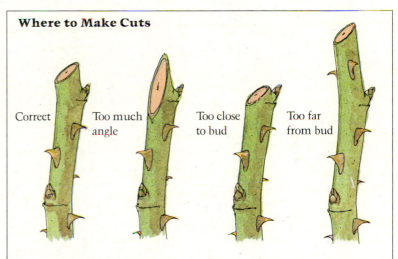

Correct   Too much angle   Too close to bud   Too far from bud

When making heading cuts on a small branch, cut on a slant about ¼" above a bud. If the cut is too close, the bud may die; if it is too far away, the resulting stub will die.

Pole saws are small, curved saws mounted on an adjustable extension pole. They are useful in cutting branches less than 2 inches in diameter up to 15 feet above the ground. Pole pruners are similar to pole saws; pruning shears, located at the end of the pole, are controlled by a pulley and rope. They are good for cutting high, thin branches. Some pole pruners feature both a saw and a pulley-operated pruner. When using the pruner, take care not to injure the bark with the saw; if necessary detach the saw temporarily. The pole has a hook, which can be used to pull down any entangled branches. When pruning near power lines, use wood or fiberglass poles.

A chain saw may be necessary to cut through large branches or trunks. They are available in many sizes and types—gasoline, electric, or hydraulically powered. Use them with caution! Climbing into a tree with a chain saw is extremely dangerous. It may be best to save this chore for a professional arborist.

WHEN TO PRUNE

In general the best time to prune any woody plant is just before new growth starts. Pruning in late winter or early spring while a plant is dormant won't adversely affect its vigor; but pruning at other times can rob it of stored food energy. Severe pruning during or just after active growth in spring only wastes stored energy. Such pruning can dwarf a plant and is not recommended unless a dwarfing effect is the goal, such as for a bonsai.

Photosynthesis is most active during summer, when plants produce abundant food and new growth. As the days shorten in late summer, growth slows and sugars accumulate in the leaves. Before the foliage drops the food moves from the leaves into the woody branches. Pruning in fall or early winter depletes the stored food reserves needed to initiate spring growth. Since many decay fungi produce spores in fall, that is also the time when open wounds are most likely to become infected with decay rot. Later in the dormant season, sugars move farther down the plant and are less likely to be disturbed. Pruning at that time doesn't waste stored energy and cuts heal more quickly.

New growth can be directed by pruning in late winter or early spring before leaves appear. It is easy at this time of year to examine the structural arrangement of the branches of deciduous trees and shrubs and plan pruning strategies. Dormant season pruning is good for the plant and the gardener. It is a time when few other garden chores make demands and the outdoor activity is excellent exercise.

However, there are cases in which pruning should be done during the growing season. If spring-flowering shrubs are pruned in winter, the flower buds will be removed and the plants won't blossom that spring. The spring flowering trees and shrubs that bloom on the previous season's growth should be pruned immediately after flowering, but before leaves fully expand. Summer-blooming plants, which usually bloom on the current-season's growth, can be pruned in winter without danger of removing flower buds; in fact, dormant-season pruning will stimulate more flowers. (See "Pruning Deciduous Shrubs and Vines," page 43, for more information on timing.)

Midsummer pruning has a dwarfing effect on plants. Removing summer foliage reduces

photosynthesis, resulting in less food reserves for the following spring's growth. Summer pruning is appropriate for slowing the vigorous growth of an immature fruit tree so that it will begin bearing. Dwarf fruit trees especially are subjected to frequent light pruning during the summer. This controls their shape and avoids overly vigorous spring growth. Summer pruning will prevent an extremely vigorous tree from responding to heavy pruning with a burst of water sprouts and suckers. Summer pruning is also recommended for restricting growth of a tree or shrub that has reached a desired height and spread. However, because wounds will not callus over as rapidly as during the late dormant season, it's best to keep summer pruning cuts small and save heavy shaping for winter.

The worst time to prune is right after leaves emerge in spring. Stored energy has

Let common sense guide you when it comes to pruning safely—don't take chances. When using a ladder, be careful that it has a sure footing. When reaching into a tree or shrub with one hand to hold a branch, protect the hand from being nicked with the clippers by wearing a leather glove on that hand.

powered the initiation and expansion of the new foliage, but the leaves have not yet begun to accumulate food to replenish the supply. Bud break in spring is also the time of greatest root growth, another heavy drain on stored reserves. Until food manufacture equals or surpasses food utilization, the plant can ill afford to lose foliage. In addition, the tissue beneath the bark is soft during the spring growth; it is easy to tear the bark when pruning.

With judgment and moderation, some pruning can be done at any time. However, pruning between leafing out and midsummer can produce an especially strong, harmful dwarfing effect on plants. Dead and dying branches, suckers, and water sprouts should be removed anytime they become apparent. And, of course, removing a few stragglers or branches that are out of line during the growing season won't do much harm.

SAFETY PRECAUTIONS

Working with sharp pruning saws, electric shears or a chain saw can be dangerous. Handling these tools while on a ladder or perched in a tree compounds the chance of a mishap. Always use common sense when wielding these sharp tools.

Before attempting to prune from a ladder, look up for electrical lines and dead or hanging branches. Consider where the branch will fall when it is cut or dropped from the tree—be sure it won't fall on anyone or knock into the ladder. Be safe. Use a stepladder or tie an extension ladder securely to the tree and keep one hand on it and one on the saw. Station someone on the ground as a lookout and safety checker.

Wear nonskid rubber-soled shoes, snug clothing, and leather gloves. When using a chain saw, wear leather boots. Professionals wear hard hats and protective glasses because it is easy to bump into a branch and scratch an eye or lose a contact lens.

WHEN TO HIRE A PROFESSIONAL

There are many reasons to hire a professional for pruning chores. You may not have enough time to take care of extensive hedges or shrubbery yourself. Or you may lack the skill or equipment for major pruning jobs. Tree pruning can be dangerous and often should be

left to a professional, especially if the branches to be removed are heavy or high up. It is safer in many cases to call a professional tree-care company with expertise, equipment, and insurance coverage.

Although extensive professional tree and shrub pruning can be expensive, don't let the cost alone deter you if the price is not out of reach. Landscape plants represent a considerable investment and add to the value of a home. Properly pruned trees and shrubs will be more attractive, healthier, longer-lived, and less susceptible to storm damage. They are worth taking care of properly. Pruning is the most important way to control their size and maintain an investment that appreciates every year.

In hiring a professional, make sure that the person is knowledgeable, reputable, and experienced. Not all those who advertise themselves as tree- or garden-care specialists actually possess the skill needed to do the job properly.

Use the same care as you would to find a family doctor, dentist, or lawyer. Ask for references and addresses where the company has recently pruned trees and shrubs. Drive past, inspect the work, and follow up with a phone call to the homeowner.

Before making a decision, ask questions to find out how knowledgeable the firm is. See if they can explain the following.

☐ The role of apical dominance in plants.

☐ The location and importance of the swollen branch collar.

☐ Thinning, heading, and shearing.

☐ The pruning methods that they will use.

If the firm is knowledgeable, the next step is to evaluate its level of professionalism.

☐ Will it remove the brush after pruning?

☐ Is it a member of nursery, landscape, or arborist associations?

☐ Are the equipment and vehicles clean, well maintained, and marked with the firm's name and address?

☐ Does the firm have a pesticide operator's license if spraying is needed?

☐ Is it insured for liability and accidents?

☐ Has the firm been in business for at least several years?

☐ Have the owner and employees kept up-to-date in new research practices and methods by attending in-service training?

Pruning Deciduous Trees

When removing a branch, the position of the cut determines the pattern of new growth that follows. Learn how to develop a strong set of scaffold branches, remove heavy branches, and thin out or reduce the size of a large tree.

Trees are one of the most important elements in a home landscape. Tall-growing trees cast welcome shade and soften the skyline; lower-growing flowering trees decorate the yard with delightful blossoms and provide a lower canopy of foliage. Shade trees and flowering trees are often deciduous—they drop their leaves during the dormant season. Although they don't need much pruning if they are planted in the correct spot (not too close to the house, driveway, or other structures), deciduous trees grow more vigorously and develop a sturdier branching structure with some corrective pruning throughout their lives.

Fast-growing and marginally hardy trees require more intensive pruning. Avoid future problems by planting species and cultivars of trees that demand the least care and are suitable for the climate. Avoid any trees that produce weak wood, narrow crotches (branching angles), or surface roots or that are susceptible to diseases or insects.

This chapter deals with pruning both young and older trees. The pruning begun at planting time and continued during the next several years determines the strength and shape of the branch structure. As the tree grows older, it is often necessary to prune off branches that are too low, growing in the wrong direction, or damaged by storms. It is also important to learn how to properly reduce the size of a tree that has grown too large for its place in the landscape.

Deciduous trees are best pruned in late winter when their branching structure is clearly visible and any errant branches are easily spotted.

TREE GROWTH PATTERNS

By knowing something about the basic structure of a tree, you can prune more intuitively. The tree trunk supports the major limbs, which bear branches, leaves, flowers, and fruit. Inside the trunk and branches are two rings of tissue that act as pipelines to carry nutrients and water throughout the tree. The inner ring carries water and minerals from the roots to the branches, leaves, flowers, and fruit. The outer ring, just beneath the bark, carries sugars manufactured in the leaves to the rest of the plant.

A tree trunk supports the branches, which in turn serve as a framework for the leaves.

Anatomy of a Tree

Leader · Spur · Leaves · Flowers · Fruit · Scaffold (main) branch · Lateral (side) branch · Trunk · Roots

Branches have identifying names depending upon their position on the trunk. The leader is the central branch, seemingly a continuation of the main trunk. (Some trees develop a single main trunk for life; others begin with a single leader but develop multiple leaders as they mature.) Scaffold branches are the main side branches. Lateral branches arise horizontally from scaffold branches. Spurs are short twigs or branches that bear flowers and fruit. Water sprouts are fast-growing shoots that develop from latent buds located on the trunk or branches. Suckers are vigorous shoots that grow from roots or the base of the trunk.

Food is manufactured in plant leaves by the process of photosynthesis. Powered by energy from sunlight, the leaves combine carbon dioxide and water to form simple sugars and complex carbohydrates. This is the source of energy for all plant growth processes.

Roots have multiple functions. In addition to absorbing water and essential minerals, roots anchor the tree and store food reserves.

Tree Shapes

Deciduous trees naturally grow in dense stands in the forest. As these trees crowd each other and shade the lower branches of neighboring trees, they develop a narrow, upright growth habit. However, when a forest tree is grown in the open—such as in the middle of a lawn—unpressured by competition, its crown is no longer limited to an upright shape and can become broader and more spreading. Many species that normally form a strong central leader in a forest form multiple leaders as they mature in a home landscape. These trees may require pruning and shaping to encourage a sturdy branch structure.

Trees are subject to the control of apical dominance (see pages 11 and 12). The tallest and most vertical branches, in particular, concentrate hormones in the terminal bud. These hormones inhibit the growth of the current season's lateral buds for a year or more. The varying strength of apical dominance from species to species is the reason different trees have different shapes. Those with a prominent central leader, such as pin oak, sweet gum, and tulip tree, are governed by strong apical control. The leader outpaces growth of lateral branches to produce a pyramidal form. Eventually even these trees reach maturity, a

time when apical dominance diminishes and the pyramidal appearance of the young tree gives way to a round-topped shape.

Many trees, including maple, linden, oak, and crab apple, have a rounded shape with several or many codominant stems. Although apical dominance is strong during the first years, control over lateral shoots quickly weakens. The laterals are free to grow rapidly, often overtaking the leader and creating a multiple-trunked tree with a rounded and spreading habit.

All trees develop characteristic mature shapes or silhouettes when grown in the open. They may be vase-shaped like the American elm or roundheaded like the European linden. Still others may have wide-spreading horizontal branches like the white oak or cascading branches like the weeping willow. When pruning a tree, you should know what its natural shape is meant to be and try to maintain that form while selecting the strongest branches.

PRUNING YOUNG AND NEWLY PLANTED TREES

Pruning a tree when it is newly planted and during its first few years in the landscape will not only ensure its development into a desirable shape, but will also prevent more drastic

corrective pruning as the tree ages. Early pruning is easier for the gardener and healthier for the tree. Removing poorly positioned branches leaves a much smaller wound on a young tree than on a mature tree. Removing the same branches after they have been allowed to grow large means more expense, greater disfigurement, a longer time for the wound to close over, and a greater chance of infection by wood decay fungi.

In purchasing a young tree, care should be taken to choose one with a strong trunk. To maximize land utilization nurseries often grow trees close together, almost as if in a forest. Because they are protected from the wind, these trees do not develop sturdy trunks. If transplanted into an open area, they are prone to breaking in strong winds. On the other hand, trees that are allowed to sway in the wind actually develop stronger trunks that last a lifetime. Look for a tree that was grown with enough space; identify it by a trunk that is wider at the base, tapering upward to a full set of lower branches. A sturdy tree like this will bend without breaking.

Try to choose a tree that will remain upright without staking. Those without sufficient trunk taper may need to be staked. In that case, do not rigidly stake or guy-wire the

Left: The tulip tree, with its towering, arrow-straight trunk, is a good example of a tree that tends to form a single leader. Right: The English oak tends to form a massive, short trunk that branches into many leaders, creating a large rounded head.

Corrective Pruning of a Headed Nursery Tree

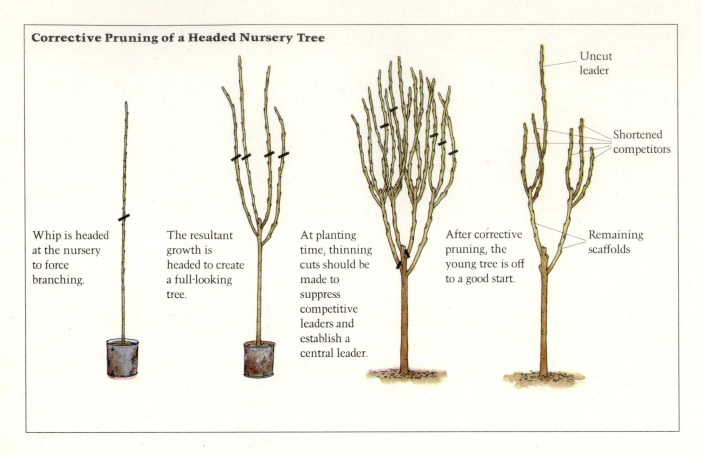

Whip is headed at the nursery to force branching.

The resultant growth is headed to create a full-looking tree.

At planting time, thinning cuts should be made to suppress competitive leaders and establish a central leader.

After corrective pruning, the young tree is off to a good start.

Uncut leader

Shortened competitors

Remaining scaffolds

tree; allow it to sway in the wind so it can develop a strong stem taper. Tie the tree to the stake with a single tie, at the lowest spot that will hold the tree upright. Prune the crown to reduce the weight of branches and foliage so they can better resist the wind. If the tree is tall and the location very windy, a second tie and a taller stake may be needed to keep the tree from breaking off above the tie.

The stake is a temporary crutch to be used only until the trunk is strong enough to support the tree. Remove the stake as soon as possible.

Nurseries often head young trees to 5 or 6 feet high to force the development of lateral side branches so the tree looks bushier and more appealing to the customer. Frequently, the new shoots grow from directly below the cut, the result of the sudden loss of apical dominance. As the tree grows, the cluster of terminal shoots often develops into more than one leader. Such a tree needs some corrective pruning to maintain a central leader (see below).

Why Prune a Newly Planted Tree?

Some corrective pruning is required on newly planted trees in order to develop a good branching structure. This holds true even if the tree is supposed to grow rapidly to form a

screen or produce shade—and despite the fact that corrective and other types of pruning cuts potentially dwarf the tree by reducing the amount of food-manufacturing foliage.

Horticulturists once recommended trimming branches of newly planted trees to one quarter to one third of their total length to compensate for roots lost when the tree was dug from the nursery field. Roots absorb water, which moves up the tree into the leaves and is lost to the air in a process called transpiration. If the reduced root system cannot absorb sufficient water, leaves may wilt and fail to grow properly. By pruning off branches and foliage, the horticulturists thought to reduce the demand for water. This practice is now outdated.

Research has shown that as the terminal leaf buds of sugar maples expand they release hormones that initiate root growth. (This phenomenon undoubtedly applies to other trees as well.) Overzealous pruning of a third of the branches to compensate for root loss slows the growth of new roots and delays the tree's establishment in the landscape. Heavy pruning after transplanting also causes the tree to develop fewer, larger leaves; this limits food production, slowing recovery and dwarfing the new growth. If pruning is necessary, use thinning cuts so that only a few terminal buds are removed.

Adequate moisture is critical when new leaves emerge because they must function effectively to restore energy reserves depleted during the flush of new growth in spring. Rather than severely pruning to reduce the risk of inadequate moisture uptake, it is better to take cultural measures to reduce water stress. Transplant while the tree is dormant—after leaf drop in fall or before the buds break in spring. Both spring and fall are generally times of abundant rainfall, a benefit to the struggling tree. Water the tree well for two growing seasons after planting; keep in mind that moisture loss is more rapid in high temperatures, winds, bright sun, and low humidity than when the weather is cloudy.

This doesn't mean that trees should not be pruned at planting time; they should, but not severely. The most important reason for pruning a young tree is to encourage its natural shape. At planting time and during the first several years, remove only undesirable and broken branches. Allow enough foliage to produce plenty of food for tree growth. Also select some of the primary scaffold branches after planting, if this has not been done in the nursery. Follow a light, corrective training program to help develop a strong central leader and good branching structure.

Developing a Leader

The first task is to determine which branch is or should be the main leader. If several are growing upright in the center, select the most vigorous or most central as the leader. Remove or shorten the competing branches to prevent the formation of a split leader, which is inherently weak and susceptible to breaking during storms. To shorten and subdue the growth of a potential competitor without removing it entirely, cut the branch back by one third to one half of its length to a lateral twig, thin to a small side branch, or head it to a leaf or bud. This removes the terminal bud and arrests the upright growth pattern.

The greatest mistake in pruning a young tree is to prune the leader—except if it is thinned to a lateral, which would then assume apical dominance. The loss of apical control also means the loss of the main leader upon

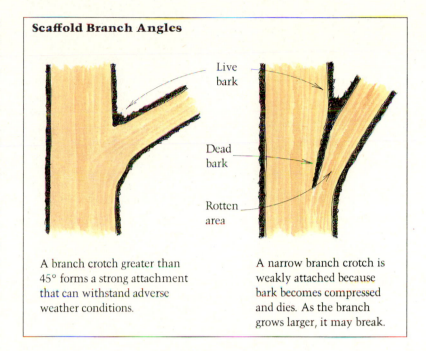

Scaffold Branch Angles

Live bark

Dead bark

Rotten area

A branch crotch greater than 45° forms a strong attachment that can withstand adverse weather conditions.

A narrow branch crotch is weakly attached because bark becomes compressed and dies. As the branch grows larger, it may break.

which the primary scaffold branches arise. Seldom is there any justification for cutting back or removing the leader of a young tree. Even in trees that form multiple leaders with age, encouraging a strong central leader when the tree is young results in a sturdier branch structure later.

Selecting Scaffolds

Select the lowest branches to be kept permanently. The permanent lateral scaffolds, the principal branches of the tree, should arise from the central leader. Depending upon the height of the tree, none of the present branches may actually remain when the tree is mature; keep in mind that a tree adds height to its top as it grows and branches remain at the same level although they increase in diameter. Branches on most trees should not be so low that it is impossible to sit or walk beneath them. The lowest limbs on trees overhanging a driveway or street must allow clearance for a delivery truck.

The best branches to select for main scaffolds emerge from the trunk at an angle greater than 45 degrees. These spreading lateral branches are strongly attached to the trunk with connective wood and have desirably small branch bark ridges, which are naturally weak areas on a tree (see page 15). As branches with angles narrower than 45 degrees grow larger, the bark of the trunk and branch becomes sandwiched into the crotch,

Branch Spacing

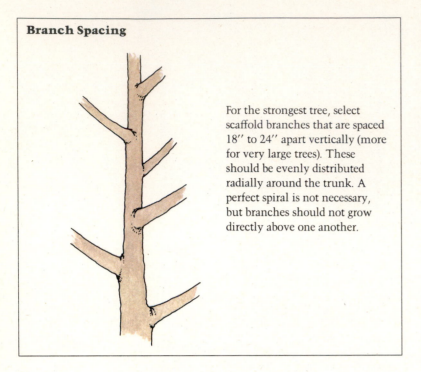

For the strongest tree, select scaffold branches that are spaced 18″ to 24″ apart vertically (more for very large trees). These should be evenly distributed radially around the trunk. A perfect spiral is not necessary, but branches should not grow directly above one another.

forming a large branch bark ridge and a weak attachment. As these branches grow heavy with age, the angle begins to spread and the crotch can split apart at the branch bark ridge in windstorms. With the exception of trees that have distinctly narrow and upright habits like the Lombardy poplar or columnar cultivars of maples, remove or subdue any potential scaffolds with narrow angles of attachment.

Strive to keep the vertical distance between scaffolds 10 to 24 inches apart in young trees. Large trees naturally may assume several feet between scaffolds. Select branches that radiate in alternating positions to avoid shading those positioned below and to eliminate competition for food and water. An ideal pattern is five to seven branches emerging from the trunk in an ascending circle that rotates once or twice. Nature is rarely this orderly so plan ahead and mark branches to keep and branches to subdue or cut out as the tree grows.

As the tree matures and begins to express its characteristic branching pattern, it assumes one of two basic forms: central leader with a pyramidal shape and one main trunk or multiple leader with trunks equaling or exceeding the main leader.

On newly planted or young trees, do not remove all the branches below any permanent scaffolds. Leave these temporarily to protect and shade the trunk and contribute to food production. Maintaining these low branches for several years adds to the width of the base of the trunk and encourages the well-defined upward taper of a strong and flexible tree. Although these branches aren't removed, their growth should be subdued. Continue to do this every year until the branches can be removed entirely. A good time to eliminate these temporary branches is when their diameter reaches about ½ inch. A cut this size closes in about one year.

When pruning small branches with a pruning saw, hold the branch in one hand and use the other to cut along the slanting outside edge of the collar. Make saw cuts with an upstroke to avoid injuring bark in the crotch between the trunk and branch.

Corrective Pruning of Lateral Branches

Whenever the trunk or a branch forks, the main branch should have a larger diameter than the other or the crotch may split. If the diameter of a side branch is equal to or greater than the diameter of the main trunk or parent branch, subdue its growth by pruning it back with a thinning cut by one third of its total length.

Training young and recently transplanted trees will take several years of light pruning. The tree benefits when a branch is removed gradually over several seasons rather than being cut off abruptly. Most branching problems in older trees are due to lack of proper pruning when the tree was young.

PRUNING NEEDS OF OLDER TREES

If correctly pruned when young, large trees generally require less pruning than most other woody plants. However, they may require occasional removal of dead or dying branches. As a shade tree grows in height and spread, it may be necessary to control its size, reduce excess shade, or prevent branches from rubbing against each other, wires, buildings, or vehicles. Removing weak branches arising from the trunk at a narrow angle also reduces the possibility of branches breaking in storms or of the trunk splitting as the tree matures.

When pruning young or mature trees, do not leave the stub of a branch after pruning.

Stubs do not callus over and can open the tree to decay-causing microorganisms. It is just as important not to make a flush cut and remove the swollen branch collar. The collar, which is part of the trunk, forms a natural protective chemical barrier that restricts the invasion of wood decay-causing organisms (see pages 14 and 15). The short collar that remains will eventually disappear as the tree grows larger. This technique of removing a branch is known as natural target pruning.

Maintaining the Leader

Avoid cutting off or heading the main leader or any of the multiple leaders of a mature tree unless it is essential for reducing the tree's height. Heading the leader eliminates apical dominance and produces vigorous, upright growth just behind the cut. The new shoots are weakly attached and easily broken. If it is necessary to prune a leader, cut back to a lateral branch with an equal or one-third smaller diameter. The side branch then assumes apical dominance. Initially the new leader bends to assume the position of the original leader, but in a few years this bend is no longer noticeable.

Removing a Competing Leader

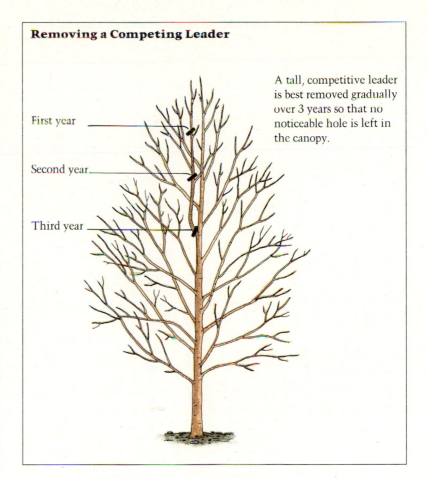

First year

Second year

Third year

A tall, competitive leader is best removed gradually over 3 years so that no noticeable hole is left in the canopy.

Pollarding

Pollarding is a method of pruning back large trees to keep them small. The main branches of a pollarded tree are headed to the same spot on the primary branches near the main trunk once a year, usually in late winter. Vigorous upright stems arise from near the pruning cut. This forms a dense canopy of leaves and young branches during the growing season. Eventually the large branch ends form knobby, club-like stubs, which look strange when the trees are leafless.

This high-maintenance form of pruning can be used to give a small but formal appearance to large-growing trees. Many of the London plane trees along the narrow streets of San Francisco are pollarded. This keeps them within bounds on the city streets. Trees in Europe are also commonly pollarded. Actually, the practice was developed centuries ago in Europe as a way to grow and harvest firewood to make charcoal without killing a tree.

Pollarded sycamore trees are a common sight along San Francisco streets.

Pleaching

Branches can be pleached, which literally means woven, to create an allée or arbor. Almost any tree with strong, flexible branches that bend without breaking is suitable for this purpose. Beech and apple trees are ideal.

Build a framework of vertical and horizontal metal pipes or wood to support the branches over a walkway. Then plant a row of young trees next to the vertical posts on each side of the walk. Tie the main trunk to the horizontal support and bend it over the supports when it grows tall enough. Head the tip of the leader so that side branches develop; tie them to the overhead framework and interweave them with branches from the other side to form a leaf tunnel or allée.

Make an easy-to-build square or rectangular pleached arbor using four vertical supports of 3-inch galvanized pipe, cut to the desired height. Make the distance between the vertical posts appropriate for the size of the garden. Connect the four posts with an overhead frame of 2-inch pipe, spaced at equal intervals and crossed to make nine squares. As the

trees at each post grow, remove any lateral shoots from the trunks. Bend and tie the vertical branches to the overhead pipe frame, interweaving them through and around to form a canopy of leaves.

Eventually some branches will graft together to support the arbor; the metal frame can then be removed. Maintain

Ironwood trees, pleached to form an elegant arbor, shade the walk and sitting areas in the garden of Dumbarton Oaks museum in Washington, D.C.

a mature pleached arbor by removing lateral branches from the trunk to allow light to penetrate to inside leaves.

To remove a competing leader, gradually cut it back rather than remove it entirely the first year. Thin out approximately one third the length of a competing leader each year for three years; this will slow it down without causing the tree to lose vigor. In trees that usually produce multiple leaders as they mature—such as maples, oaks, and lindens—subdue competing leaders by removing one third of the length of the large branches; this can be done in trees up to 15 years old. Subduing competing leaders this way slows their growth and encourages the tree to develop a stronger main leader with scaffold branches attached at more secure angles. As the tree matures, multiple leaders may form but they will be less dominant than the principal leader and the tree's structure will be better able to withstand storms.

Proper Timing
The best time to prune deciduous trees is late in the dormant season—late winter or early spring—before new growth begins and while

the branch structure is easy to observe. Callus tissue, which closes over wounds and pruning cuts, grows most quickly from early spring to midsummer and facilitates closing of dormant-season pruning cuts. However, trees such as maple, dogwood, birch, and elm leak sap from pruning wounds made in late winter or early spring. Although the flow is not harmful and soon abates, it can be uncomfortable to see and work around. A suitable alternate time for pruning these trees is midsummer, when growth has slowed. Spring-flowering trees, which bear flower buds all winter, can be lightly thinned in late winter with some loss of bloom or pruned immediately after they flower but before their leaves mature.

Thinning Cuts
Thinning, the pruning method to use for most trees, results in a more open shape and encourages the growth of interior branches. Thin crowded branches, branches that are rubbing or likely to rub against each other, and branches aiming toward the interior of

the tree rather than to the outside. It is possible to thin a great number of branches without changing the natural branching pattern or overall appearance of the tree. A properly thinned tree is healthier and more resistant to wind damage. It casts a less dense shadow, more suitable for growing a lawn or shade-loving garden plants.

Using a pruning saw, remove a branch at its point of origin on a parent stem, being careful to cut just to the outside of the swollen branch collar (see page 14). Or cut the branch back to where it makes a Y with a strong lateral branch. Choose a side branch that is growing in a desirable direction and one with a diameter at least two thirds the size of the branch being removed. Thinning cuts should be used in each of the pruning methods described below.

Removing Large Branches

Branches that are rubbing against the house or growing where they shouldn't be can be thinned or totally removed. Avoid heading them back to a stub; not only is this unsightly, but the resulting growth, which originates near the stub, will quickly become a problem.

Remove a branch too large to hold in one hand with three separate cuts; otherwise the weight of the cut branch will tear a strip of bark from the tree (see illustration below).

Removing Crossed Branches

In addition to inevitably injuring one another, rubbing or crossing branches may lead to limb decay and death. Any of the three pruning operations mentioned below can be used to remove a crossing limb without, it is hoped, leaving a large hole in the outline of a tree.

Step 1, top left: To remove a large, heavy limb, first cut one third of the way through the underside of the branch, about 1 foot from the trunk.
Step 2, top right: From the top of the branch, make a cut that is about 2 inches farther from the trunk than the first cut; the branch will snap off without tearing the bark.
Step 3, bottom left: Remove the remaining stub by cutting outside the branch bark ridge and along the outer edge of the branch collar.

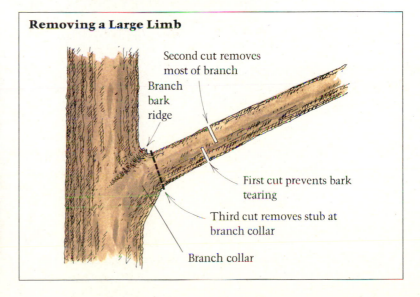

Removing a Large Limb

Second cut removes most of branch

Branch bark ridge

First cut prevents bark tearing

Third cut removes stub at branch collar

Branch collar

MAJOR CORRECTIVE MEASURES FOR MATURE TREES

The National Arborist Association has established the following terminology to define specific pruning practices on large trees.

Crown Lifting

Lifting the crown or canopy of a tree involves removing lower branches that create an obstruction or hazard. This results in a tree with high scaffold branches. The crown of a tall shade tree may be lifted if the branches overhang a parking area or roof, or to accommodate small flowering trees beneath the boughs as in a woodland setting. Other reasons to lift a crown are to provide more light for gardens and lawn below or to open up a view. As with training a young tree, it's better to lift branches gradually over a period of several years. Thinning to upright-growing laterals is a good temporary measure.

Crown Thinning and Reduction

Crown thinning—removing selected branches throughout a canopy—allows more light to enter the interior of the tree, reduces wind resistance and weight in trees with weak branches or poorly anchored roots, and emphasizes an unusual or picturesque branching pattern. Usually branches about 1 inch in diameter are thinned back to larger lateral branches.

Crown reduction or size control is necessary when a tree grows beyond the space allotted for it in the landscape, reaches into utility wires, or hangs over buildings. Begin to control size before the tree reaches its mature height and spread. Gradually thinning the tallest branches over a period of several years accomplishes the goal. Continue to thin periodically to maintain the tree at a smaller than normal size. Trees may also be reduced in height and spread by drop crotching.

Drop Crotching

Drop crotching is used to reduce the overall size of a tree. The main trunk, scaffolds, and lateral branches can all be cut back. Thin each to the next lower crotch, where the branch divides from the parent stem. The size of the remaining branch should be two thirds or more the diameter of the branch removed so that it can establish apical dominance. If

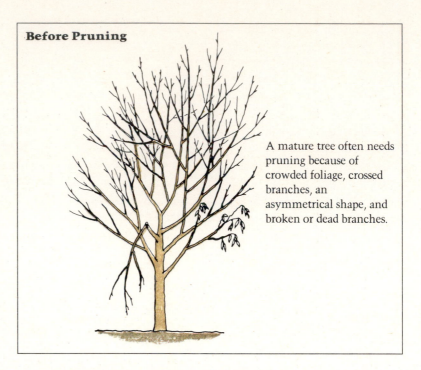

Before Pruning

A mature tree often needs pruning because of crowded foliage, crossed branches, an asymmetrical shape, and broken or dead branches.

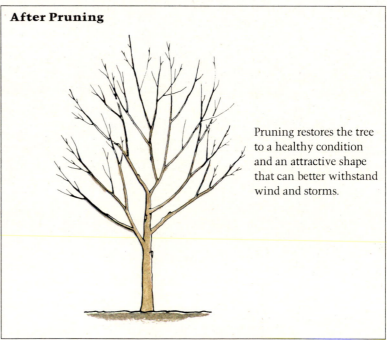

After Pruning

Pruning restores the tree to a healthy condition and an attractive shape that can better withstand wind and storms.

the drop crotch is made to a branch that is too small, the cut reacts like a heading cut and results in dense, weak, multiple shoots emerging below the cut.

To drop crotch an entire tree, start from the top and work down, exercising skill and judgment to preserve the natural growth habit and branching pattern. With proper pruning, new growth will arise from the terminal bud of the remaining branches and casual observers will not be able to detect that the greatly reduced tree was pruned.

Crown Thinning

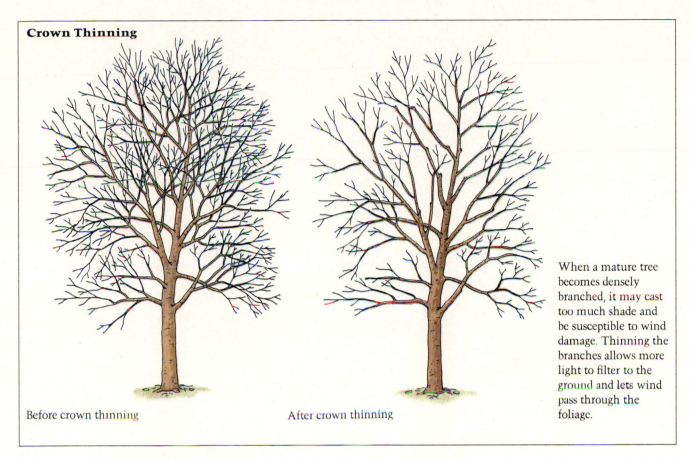

Before crown thinning

After crown thinning

When a mature tree becomes densely branched, it may cast too much shade and be susceptible to wind damage. Thinning the branches allows more light to filter to the ground and lets wind pass through the foliage.

Drop Crotching

Before drop crotching

After drop crotching

A tree that has become too tall for its landscape purpose can be made smaller without destroying its shape by drop crotching. Dramatic thinning cuts remove many of the major branches where they divide into secondary branches.

REPAIRING STORM DAMAGE

What should be done to a seriously storm-damaged tree? Is it better to remove the tree altogether or patch up what is left? In many cases, one of the pruning methods described above can be used to restore the tree's health and appearance—a damaged leader can be removed by drop crotching, for instance. In many cases, professional help may be needed to repair the damage.

To decide if a seriously damaged tree is worth saving, consult a professional arborist, who can evaluate the tree by its species, location, and contribution to the landscape, as well as estimate the cost for pruning, repairing, or replacement. If the loss affects the property value, a professional arborist can determine casualty loss to submit to the insurance company.

Do not neglect a damaged tree. If branches have been broken or twisted or if they hang from the tree, trim them off with a thinning cut if possible. An arborist can remove large broken branches and reduce the crown to restore the tree's symmetry. An arborist can also strengthen weakened branches with cables and bracing. Prompt attention can help the tree close its injuries, but neglecting the damage may mean that wood-rotting organisms gain a foothold.

Good cultural practices—such as irrigating, mulching, fertilizing, and managing pests—can reduce stress on a damaged tree until it recovers. However, avoid overstimulation of new growth with high-nitrogen fertilizers. These may force the tree to use reduced food reserves for foliage rather than root growth and wound closing. Fertilize and irrigate in moderation.

Pruning Under Utility Wires

Tree limbs can rub against utility wires and even fall on them, cutting off service during storms. Electrical utility companies are responsible for maintaining the trees around their lines. In some communities they have a reputation for disfiguring trees; in other communities environmentally conscious companies employ proper and careful pruning methods.

Some electric companies shear or stub all tree branches beneath their lines, believing this is the fastest—and least expensive—method to remove interfering branches. In reality, indiscriminate heading and stubbing produces many vigorous, fast-growing vertical sprouts, called suckers, which eat up the headspace clearance within two growing seasons.

Knowledgeable utilities prefer to thin branches. On trees growing directly beneath power lines, workers will drop crotch the terminal leader to a lateral side branch, one third smaller in diameter. Lateral branches growing off the terminal are thinned less severely, directing normal new growth away from overhead wires, but still maintaining a natural tree shape.

The same lateral pruning methods can be used on a tree growing to the side of an electric line. By pruning branches overhanging the lines back to upward shoots, and branches growing below to downward shoots, the tree will grow away from the lines, leaving a hole for them while maintaining a natural shape.

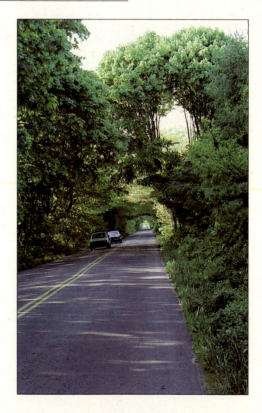

Branches that interfere with utility lines can be pruned and their growth directed to form a hole in the canopy of the tree through which the lines can pass.

SALVAGING BADLY PRUNED TREES

Restoring a badly pruned or neglected tree to its natural shape may take several years, but its appearance will be greatly improved. Usually trees suffer from having been headed, resulting in multiple vertical branches. Begin by reducing the number of verticals to one, two, or three on each limb and thin these to a lateral branch. With fewer branches, more light can penetrate to the interior of the tree and wind resistance will be reduced. Although these verticals are weakly attached, the connection strengthens with each growing season as a new layer of wood surrounds the branch collar.

Remove badly crossed branches by cutting them off at their origins, even if this leaves a hole in the tree canopy. This hole should fill in within several years. When a badly pruned tree is corrected, decay may be discovered in the branch stubs. If so, make thinning cuts back to sound wood.

HIRING AN ARBORIST

With large shade and flowering trees, most homeowners wisely limit themselves to removing small branches that are easily reached from the ground with a pole saw or with a handheld saw from a step ladder. It's best to leave the removal of larger overhead branches and work that involves climbing into a tree with a chain saw to the commercial arborist. Using a chain saw when climbing a tree or ladder, where footing and balance are uncertain, is very dangerous. A reputable arborist is trained in climbing and is properly equipped and insured.

Consider calling in an arborist in the following circumstances:

☐ When feeling uncomfortable and unsure about the job that must be done.

☐ When the branch to be cut is heavy enough to damage a roof or fence if it falls.

☐ When a chain saw is needed to remove a branch high in a tree.

Professional tree care can be expensive, but price isn't the only criterion. A cut-rate pruning job may do more harm than good! Be sure the firm or individual is knowledgeable and trustworthy. In many cases, especially following hurricanes and tornadoes, anyone with a chain saw and a pick-up truck becomes a self-proclaimed tree-care professional. The questions on page 19 are a good way to determine the qualifications of tree-care firms.

The National Arborist Association (174 Rural Route 101, Bedford Station, Box 238, Bedford, NH 03102) may be able to provide a list of members in your area.

This flowering cherry tree has been incorrectly pruned and then neglected. Crossed branches, water sprouts, and stubs need to be removed.

Using a pole saw with a clipper makes it easy to remove the errant branches.

After corrective pruning, the tree is more open and branches are growing in the right directions without interfering with one another.

Acer palmatum (Japanese maple)

Acer platanoides (Norway maple)

DECIDUOUS TREE PRUNING ENCYCLOPEDIA

This encyclopedic guide describes how to prune many of the most commonly planted deciduous trees. The pruning information for a particular species is applicable to most of its cultivars, but as with all generalities there are exceptions; the text tries to point these out when they occur.

The trees are listed alphabetically by their botanical names. To find out a plant's botanical name look up the common name in the index, which will list the botanical name and the page on which the tree is discussed.

Acer buergeranum
Trident maple

See *Acer ginnala*

Acer campestre
Hedge maple

See *Acer ginnala*

Acer ginnala
Amur maple

Often multiple-trunked and spreading, these maples rarely exceed 30 feet tall.

How to prune   Remove lower branches to allow room for walking under tree; keep lower branches for a bushy effect. These strong trees seldom require anything but corrective pruning such as removing crossing or low branches.

When to prune   Late dormant season (typical bleeding of maples at this time doesn't harm tree).

Acer negundo
Ash-leaved maple, box elder

Popular in the Midwest, this wide-spreading, fast-growing tree reaches 50 feet.

How to prune   Because the box elder has brittle wood, direct early efforts to developing strong, wide-angled, and well-spaced scaffold branches. When mature, thin the crown to reduce wind resistance.

When to prune   Dormant season (typical bleeding of maples during late dormant season doesn't harm tree).

Acer palmatum
Japanese maple

This small, slow-growing tree can reach 30 feet tall and 20 feet wide. Easily maintained at any size, this is the airiest and most delicate of the maples.

How to prune   Train as a handsome single- or multiple-trunked specimen. It requires little pruning other than to encourage the natural airy layered habit.

When to prune   Dormant season (typical bleeding of maples during late dormant season doesn't harm tree).

Acer platanoides
Norway maple

Growing to 50 feet tall with a 70-foot spread, this maple is tough and hardy. A stocky tree, it has heavy branches and a dense crown.

How to prune   Retain the small shoots arising from main branches. Remove dead or crossing branches and, in areas of high winds, thin to open the crown and reduce wind resistance. Little other pruning is needed.

When to prune   Dormant season (typical bleeding of maples during late dormant season doesn't harm tree); also midsummer.

Acer rubrum
Red maple

A tree with strong wood, red maple reaches 60 to 70 feet tall. Prune it similarly to the sugar maple (see *Acer saccharum*).

Acer saccharinum
River maple, silver maple

This tree grows quickly to 60 to 100 feet. Branches are brittle and subject to storm damage.

How to prune   Prune to correct natural faults such as weak, narrow branch crotches. Try to space strong scaffold branches with wide-angled crotches along a central leader. Thin the crown of mature trees to lessen wind resistance by drop crotching.

When to prune   Dormant season; will bleed profusely if pruned after growth begins in spring.

Acer rubrum (red maple)

Albizia julibrissin (mimosa)

Betula pendula (white birch)

Acer saccharum
Sugar maple

Sugar maple is probably the best of the commonly grown maples. It grows 80 to 100 feet tall and 60 to 80 feet wide.

How to prune   Maintain a single leader for 30 to 40 feet or as long as practical. Remove crossing secondary branches and weak, tight crotches. Prune to maintain widely spaced scaffolds.

When to prune   Dormant season or midsummer.

Aesculus × carnea
Red horse chestnut

See *Aesculus hippocastanum*

Aesculus hippocastanum
Horse chestnut

Pyramidal when young, these flowering trees mature into a rounded crown with descending branches. They grow 30 to 50 feet tall.

How to prune   Prune occasionally to remove deadwood. Reduce interior branching if a mature specimen becomes

overly dense. Otherwise does not need much pruning.

When to prune   Late dormant season.

Albizia julibrissin
Mimosa, silk tree

This frequently multitrunked tree grows fast to reach 25 to 40 feet tall with an even greater spread. Its arching branches form an umbrella-like canopy. Leafs out in later spring.

How to prune   For a typical umbrella form, establish the first scaffold branches about 8 feet from the ground and thin the tree when it reaches the desired height. Since the wood is weak, thin long horizontal branches to reduce their weight.

When to prune   Late dormant season; wait until after frost danger passes in cold-winter areas.

Alnus species
Alder

Alders are fast-growing trees with potentially invasive moisture-loving roots. Most develop

straight trunks with a definite central leader, but some branch from the base becoming large shrubs.

How to prune   For a single-trunked tree, remove the low-growing branches that compete with the central leader. Remove small dead branches annually.

When to prune   Dormant season.

Amelanchier species
Serviceberry, shadbush, juneberry

These small native trees, reaching around 25 feet tall, usually have multiple trunks.

How to prune   It's best to let the natural form prevail, but if a single trunk is desired prune out all but the strongest.

When to prune   Late dormant season.

Betula nigra
Black birch, red birch, river birch

Black birch grows rapidly when young, often reaching 70 feet tall in the wild. The

conical shape becomes open and spreading with age.

How to prune   This birch can be trained as a single- or multiple-trunked tree. Prune to reveal colorful, peeling bark. Remove branches with weak crotches and dead or diseased wood.

When to prune   Late summer; will bleed profusely if pruned in spring and this can discolor the bark.

Betula pendula (also sold as B. alba and B. verrucosa)
European white birch, white birch

This weeping white-barked tree commonly grows about 40 feet tall and 20 feet wide.

How to prune   This tree does not respond well to pruning. Cut to the outside of branch collar and do not leave long stubs. Remove low-growing, dead, or diseased branches.

When to prune   Late summer; will bleed if pruned during the growing season and sap may stain the bark.

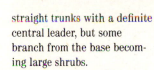

Celtis australis (hackberry)

Cercis canadensis (redbud)

Celtis occidentalis (sugarberry)

Carpinus betulus
European hornbeam

Slow-growing tree that reaches 40 to 60 feet tall at maturity. Its wood is extremely hardy, heavy, and tough. A pyramidal tree, it either forms multiple stems or has a vertical leader with laterals emerging at sharp upward angles.

How to prune　Little pruning is needed.

When to prune　Late dormant season.

Carya illinoinensis
Pecan, hickory

This tree, which produces edible nuts, grows to 60 to 100 feet tall with an equal spread.

How to prune　Space scaffold branches widely along the trunk when the tree is young. Little pruning is needed on mature trees except to remove dead or diseased wood.

When to prune　Late dormant season.

Catalpa bignonioides
Common catalpa

This fast-growing tree reaches 30 to 50 feet tall with a nearly equal spread.

How to prune　Maintain a central leader until the tree is around 12 feet tall. Then allow it to begin the characteristic extensive branching that quickly opens the crown. Left unpruned, branches will develop all the way down the trunk to the ground. Since the wood is weak, shorten the branches on older trees to reduce weight. Catalpa is tolerant of pollarding.

When to prune　Dormant season for major cuts; anytime for touch-up pruning.

Celtis australis
European nettle tree, honeyberry, lote tree, Mediterranean hackberry

See *Celtis occidentalis*

Celtis laevigata
Sugarberry, Mississippi hackberry

See *Celtis occidentalis*

Celtis occidentalis
Sugarberry, nettle tree

These species grow at a moderate rate to 50 feet or more tall and are wide spreading.

How to prune　Train major scaffold branches on a young tree to begin about 8 feet off the ground. Watch for pendulous branches and weak crotches. Mature trees seldom need pruning.

When to prune　Dormant season.

Cercidiphyllum japonicum
Katsura tree

As a single-stemmed tree, katsura can grow 60 to 100 feet tall. It is more often grown as a multitrunked specimen, reaching 30 to 60 feet tall.

How to prune　To train as a single-trunked tree, thin all competing branches. With multiple trunks the tree can develop a tremendous spread, causing branches to break. Thin branches that place excess weight on the tree.

When to prune　Late dormant season.

Cercis canadensis
Eastern redbud, Judas tree

Growing 25 to 35 feet high and wide, redbud is irregularly roundheaded. The tree is known for handsome reddish brown bark, zigzag branching, and rosy flowers that bloom on the trunk and bare branches.

How to prune　May form multiple trunks. Little pruning is required except to remove deadwood. When mature, prune to maintain the canopy shape. Minimize other pruning to avoid wounds and the risk of disease.

When to prune　Dormant season or after flowering.

Chionanthus virginicus
Fringe tree

Bearing fragrant white flowers followed by blue berries, fringe tree requires very little maintenance. It can be a small tree or large shrub, growing slowly to 12 to 20 feet tall.

How to prune　Occasional pruning only is required to develop a picturesque shape.

When to prune　Dormant season or after flowering.

Cladrastis lutea (American yellowwood)

Elaeagnus angustifolia (Russian olive)

Cornus florida (flowering dogwood)

Cladrastis lutea
American yellowwood,
yellowwood, virgilia

With a mature height of
50 feet, yellowwood begins by
growing upright and eventually spreads into a vase shape.

How to prune The wood is
somewhat brittle. Keep young
trees growing around a central
leader as long as possible and
avoid weak narrow crotches.
Prevent competition with the
leader by shortening side
branches. This will help dis-
tribute the weight of the
crown more evenly.

When to prune Dormant
season or midsummer; will
bleed if pruned in spring after
new growth appears.

Cornus florida
Dogwood, flowering dogwood

Reaching 20 to 30 feet tall,
flowering dogwood looks good
as a single- or multiple-
trunked tree. Branches spread
outward and cascade slightly.

How to prune This tree is
most beautiful left unpruned.
Don't remove low branches,
particularly in cold areas
because they shade the bark,
protecting it from temperature
extremes.

When to prune Dormant
season or summer. May bleed
if pruned in spring.

Cornus kousa
Kousa dogwood, Chinese
dogwood (var. *chinensis*)

A shrub or small tree growing
around 20 feet tall, this dogwood tends to form multiple
trunks with attractive bark.
Often strongly vase-shaped,
the tree blooms profusely in
early summer.

How to prune Generally
little pruning is required
other than to remove crossed
branches. Remove lower
branches to expose the mottled bark.

When to prune Dormant
season. May bleed if pruned
in spring.

Crataegus laevigata
English hawthorn, hawthorn

This moderately fast-growing
tree reaches 20 feet tall and
15 feet wide. Armed with
thorns, it makes an impene-
trable barrier or hedge.

How to prune Remove
water sprouts and thin the
crown. Fireblight can be a
problem; remove infected
twigs well below the deadwood. Tolerates shearing.

When to prune Dormant
season.

Elaeagnus angustifolia
Russian olive

A tough shrub or small tree,
Russian olive has an open,
airy habit. It grows rapidly,
reaching 20 feet tall.

How to prune Encourage
a strong central leader and
wide-angled scaffolds when
young. Prune some of the
branch tips to prevent the
branches from becoming too
long and prone to breaking.
The old wood contains many
dormant buds that will sprout
even after severe pruning. Tolerates shearing into a hedge.

When to prune Dormant
season or midsummer.

Fagus sylvatica
European beech, beech

See *Fagus grandifolia*

Fagus grandifolia
American beech

These slow-growing trees,
which can reach 80 feet tall,
develop a dense pyramidal
form with magnificent thick,
smooth, gray trunks.

How to prune Select one
leader if the tree does not do
this naturally. Multiple leaders may split off when older
and heavier. As the tree matures, remove lowest branches
to reveal the handsome trunk.

When to prune Dormant
season.

Fraxinus pennsylvanica
Red ash, green ash

Fast-growing to 30 to 50 feet
tall, red ash has an open,
broad oval crown.

How to prune Train when
young to develop the best
form. Thin low branches to
promote the central leader.
Select wide-angled branches as
main scaffolds. Remove lower
branches if they begin to die
back when a dense crown
develops.

When to prune Dormant
season.

Gleditsia triacanthos var. *inermis* (honey locust)

Koelreuteria paniculata (golden-rain tree)

Ginkgo biloba
Maidenhair tree, ginkgo

The growth rate of ginkgo, which can reach 100 feet tall, varies with climate. Although conical and sparsely branched when young, it becomes more dense and spreading with age. Male cultivars such as 'Autumn Gold' and 'Lakeview' are recommended.

How to prune   Ginkgo usually forms a strong central leader but if secondary leaders develop, remove them. Multiple leaders weaken mature specimens. Remove dead and diseased wood and rootstalk suckers. Old trees need little pruning.

When to prune   Late dormant season.

Gleditsia triacanthos var. inermis
Honey locust, honeyshuck, thornless honey locust

This fast-growing, round-headed tree reaches 40 to 60 feet tall.

How to prune   Improved thornless varieties are extra vigorous and may develop long new growth on twigs and branches. If this happens, thin about one third of the new growth in midsummer. Thin older trees two to four years to control overall size.

When to prune   Dormant season.

Jacaranda mimosifolia (often mislabeled as J. acutifolia)
Jacaranda

This deciduous or semievergreen tree is popular in warm climates. Open, irregular, and often multitrunked, it grows 25 to 40 feet tall.

How to prune   Train as single- or multiple-trunked tree. Thin back mature trees occasionally.

When to prune   Late dormant season.

Koelreuteria paniculata
Golden-rain tree, varnish tree

Growing 25 to 30 feet tall, this tree has wide-spreading branches.

How to prune   Very little pruning is needed. Select strong scaffold branches on a young tree. Remove any dead, diseased or poorly placed branches on an older specimen.

When to prune   Dormant season.

Laburnum × watereri 'Vossii'
Golden-chain tree, Vossii laburnum

The most popular cultivar of this dense, vase-shaped tree, which grows to 30 feet tall, bears 2-foot-long chains of yellow flowers in spring or early summer.

How to prune   To train into a tree, rub off buds along the bottom of the trunk, or it may become shrublike. Rejuvenate older trees with severe pruning. Prune annually to keep neat. Avoid making large pruning wounds, which close over slowly.

When to prune   After flowering or as late as August; will bleed profusely if pruned in early spring.

Lagerstroemia indica
Crape myrtle

Grows slowly into a multitrunked vase shape about 10 to 30 feet tall. Bears a profusion of showy flowers in late summer; has attractive bark.

How to prune   Train into a single stem if desired. Prune to enhance shape and to reveal mottled bark. Prune heavily to stimulate the growth of new wood, which bears the flowers. Remove suckers, branches, and dead or diseased wood.

When to prune   Dormant season for major cuts; touch-up pruning anytime.

Larix decidua
European larch

One of the few deciduous conifers, European larch grows 40 to 60 feet tall. Its slender pyramidal form widens with age.

How to prune   Little pruning is needed other than to limit spread by subduing bottom branches. Do not prune the central leader.

When to prune   Anytime; spring or early summer to subdue branches.

Morus alba (mulberry)

Laburnum × *watereri* 'Vossii' (golden-chain tree)

Malus floribunda (crab apple)

Liquidambar styraciflua

American sweet gum, red gum, sweet gum

This pyramidal tree with a strong central leader can grow to 90 feet tall, often forming a spreading crown with age.

How to prune   When young, space scaffolds widely along the trunk to establish a strong framework. Do not remove the central leader.

When to prune   Dormant season.

Liriodendron tulipifera

Tulip poplar, tulip tree, yellow poplar

This is a fast-growing tree to 80 feet tall with a pyramidal form and straight trunk.

How to prune   Maintain a strong central leader. Remove upright shoots that arise from major laterals.

When to prune   Late dormant season.

Malus floribunda

Crab apple, Japanese flowering crab apple

Over 50 species and varieties of this spring-flowering tree are grown in North America; size varies with the cultivar.

How to prune   Train when young with the modified central-leader method (see page 90). Thin lightly every year. Heavy, less frequent pruning may force unwanted growth. Remove suckers.

When to prune   After flowering; branches removed before spring flowering can be forced into bloom indoors.

Melia azedarach

Bead tree, Chinaberry, China tree, Texas umbrella tree, umbrella tree

Grows 30 to 50 feet tall with a slightly greater spread. Produces purple flowers followed by poisonous yellow berries.

How to prune   Little pruning is needed other than occasional removal of deadwood and crossing branches.

When to prune   Early dormant season.

Morus alba

White mulberry, mulberry

This fast-growing, wide-spreading tree reaches about 35 feet tall. Fruitless varieties are best.

How to prune   Develop a strong structure during the first three to five years. Cut back new growth 20 to 30 percent to outward-facing shoots or buds. Develop three to five scaffolds with three to five laterals each.

When to prune   Dormant season.

Nyssa sylvatica

Black tupelo, black gum, sour gum, pepperidge

This tree grows moderately fast to about 50 feet tall with a 25-foot spread.

How to prune   As the tree becomes established, remove lower branches to accommodate the pendulous habit and clear space for walking underneath.

When to prune   Dormant season.

Oxydendrum arboreum

Sourwood

This graceful, narrow tree with a rounded top and drooping branches grows slowly to 35 feet or taller.

How to prune   Little pruning is needed. Encourage a central leader, remove narrow-crotched branches, and keep branches low to the ground to help develop a strong trunk.

When to prune   Late dormant season.

Pistacia chinensis

Chinese pistachio, Chinese pistache

This handsome shade tree grows at a moderate rate to reach 50 feet tall with a nearly equal spread.

How to prune   When young, train to a single leader. Select well-spaced scaffolds, pruning to force lateral growth. When mature, thin poorly placed limbs, remove deadwood, and reduce weight on the scaffolds.

When to prune   Dormant season.

Quercus palustris (pin oak)

Prunus yedoensis (Japanese flowering cherry)

Pyrus calleryana (callery pear)

Platanus × acerifolia
Sycamore, London plane

This roundheaded tree grows rapidly to 40 to 60 feet tall. The cultivar 'Bloodgood' is recommended.

How to prune   When young, select primary scaffolds at the height necessary to allow walking underneath. Prune to maintain a central leader. After that, only occasional removal of dead branches is required. Sycamores will tolerate pollarding. (Trees are often pollarded to reduce the chance of anthracnose infection, but 'Bloodgood' is resistant to the disease.)

When to prune   Dormant season.

Prunus species and cultivars
Flowering cherry and flowering plum

These trees can grow 30 feet tall and often as wide.

How to prune   When young, prune to establish a strong framework. Choose a central leader with widely spaced

scaffolds up to a height of approximately 10 feet. Then thin back the leader. Prune to remove poorly placed limbs and water sprouts.

When to prune   Dormant season; twigs removed in early spring when buds show color will bloom indoors.

Pyrus calleryana cultivars
Bradford pear, callery pear

Growing in a formal oval shape 25 to 30 feet tall, these trees sometimes have crowded branches with narrow crotch angles.

How to prune   When young train to a central leader with widely spaced laterals. Remove most upright branches at an early age. Later prune to remove crossing limbs, closely spaced lateral scaffolds, and deadwood. Remove basal suckers.

When to prune   Dormant season.

Quercus coccinea
Scarlet oak

This tree grows to 50 to 80 feet tall with an open branching habit.

How to prune   When young train to a central leader with well-spaced scaffolds. With maturity, only occasional corrective pruning cuts are needed.

When to prune   Dormant season.

Quercus palustris
Pin oak

This fast-growing tree with a strong pyramidal shape can reach 60 to 70 feet tall. The lower branches often descend to the ground.

How to prune   Relative to other oaks, this tree requires more training when young. Develop a central leader and select high scaffolds because they tend to droop.

When to prune   Dormant season.

Quercus phellos
Willow oak

See *Quercus rubra*

Quercus rubra
Red oak, northern red oak

These oaks are fast-growing trees that can reach 90 feet.

How to prune   When young, prune to assure best scaffold placement. When mature, little pruning is needed except to remove deadwood or crossing branches or to maintain the central leader.

When to prune   Dormant season.

Robinia pseudoacacia
Black locust, yellow locust, false acacia

Fast-growing to 75 feet tall, this tree has weak wood and shallow roots. It can be toppled in storms.

How to prune   If possible maintain the central leader for the first 30 feet as multiple leaders weaken the tree. Select strong, wide-angled scaffolds that are widely spaced. Remove broken wood and root suckers. Drop crotch tall trees to reduce height and susceptibility to wind damage.

Tilia cordata 'Greenspire' (littleleaf linden)

Ulmus parvifolia (Chinese elm)

When to prune Early dormant season or mid to late summer; will bleed if pruned in spring.

Salix babylonica
Weeping willow

This fast-growing, short-lived tree reaches 45 feet tall and wide with branches cascading to the ground. The wood is brittle.

How to prune Train to a single trunk until 15 feet tall. Remove branches below this point to direct energy into the main stem. Remove deadwood as necessary.

When to prune Dormant season is best; can be done anytime.

Sophora japonica
Japanese pagoda tree, Chinese scholar tree

Dense and upright when young, becomes round and spreading with age. It is moderate-growing to 30 feet and then slow-growing to 70 feet.

How to prune When young, maintain the central leader as long as possible and select strong scaffolds. Periodically remove weight on lower branches by thinning.

When to prune Midsummer; will bleed profusely if pruned in spring.

Sorbus aucuparia
European mountain ash, quickbeam, rowan

Growing at a moderate rate to 30 feet tall, mountain ash is narrow when young and rounded in maturity.

How to prune Thin narrow, weak crotches while young to avoid considerable work as the tree ages. Leave lower branches on the trunk, but prune them constantly so they don't compete with the leader. Maintain the leader to 10 feet and select strongly connected, wide-angled scaffolds.

When to prune Dormant season.

Tilia cordata
Littleleaf linden, linden, small-leaved European linden, basswood

This formal-looking pyramidal tree, growing 30 to 50 feet tall, tends to have many crowded branches.

How to prune Maintain the central leader as long as possible and select widely spaced scaffolds. Thin branches as required to alleviate crowding. Can be trimmed as a hedge.

When to prune Dormant season.

Ulmus americana
American elm

Fast-growing to 100 feet, this once-commonly planted tree is now scarce because of Dutch elm disease. It has a beautiful vase shape with high limbs.

How to prune This elm tolerates pruning but rarely needs it. Because bark beetles carrying the Dutch elm disease breed in dying and broken branches, remove and destroy diseased wood.

When to prune Dormant season for major work; touch-up pruning anytime.

Ulmus parvifolia
Lacebark elm, evergreen Chinese elm, Chinese elm

This fast-growing tree, reaching 40 to 60 feet tall, is semi-evergreen in warm climates. It has an oval crown and attractively peeling bark.

How to prune When young train to a single leader that begins branching at about 12 feet. Thin an overcrowded crown in winter to reduce wind resistance. Thin frequently and lightly rather than occasionally and heavily to avoid a flush of unattractive growth.

When to prune Late dormant season.

Zelkova serrata
Japanese zelkova, saw-leaf zelkova

Fast-growing to 50 to 60 feet tall, zelkova is roundheaded becoming vase-shaped as the tree ages.

How to prune Maintain the central leader to at least 7 feet. Choose strong, widely spaced scaffolds.

When to prune Dormant season.

Pruning Deciduous Shrubs and Vines

Proper pruning keeps deciduous shrubs in scale with the house and garden while maintaining the plants' natural, graceful forms. Yearly thinning keeps shrubs compact and increases flowering.

Deciduous shrubs are never static. Soft new leaves unfurl in spring; soon flowers bloom, fade, and then ripen into glossy berries or handsome seedpods. Foliage colors in autumn and bare branches in winter send playful shadows across the snow. This diversity is part of the appeal of deciduous shrubs; when properly pruned, they put on an outstanding show throughout the seasons.

The way shrubs are pruned influences their shape, size, and flowering characteristics. Although proper shrub pruning techniques are not difficult to learn, information on these techniques may be hard to come by. Instructions on how to apply lawn fertilizers appear on every fertilizer bag; each pesticide container is labeled with specific directions for its use. There are adequate instructions in many gardening books for digging holes and planting bare-root, balled-and-burlapped, and container-grown plants. But seldom are pruning instructions attached to a new plant or to a pair of pruning shears. Furthermore, many older manuals on pruning are now outdated. This chapter intends to make shrub pruning an easy matter; it explains the correct ways to prune deciduous shrubs and hedges and to rejuvenate old, neglected specimens.

This gracefully arching flowering almond is eye-catching because the thinning techniques used to control its size did not alter the natural lines of the branches.

GROWTH CHARACTERISTICS

Deciduous shrubs have distinct shapes; weeping, rounded, oval, upright, spreading, and irregularly shaped shrubs can be found in most gardens. During the growing season it is primarily foliage that determines whether a shrub is coarse-, medium-, or fine-textured. When the leaves have fallen, bark and stems define the texture. An appealing planting design can be created by contrasting or echoing the texture and shape of one shrub with another. Prune to emphasize or minimize textural and shape differences.

Professional landscape designers advocate growing shrubs in groups or masses and allowing them to blend together into a bold and striking planting. Pruning methods detailed here teach how to control size while maintaining the natural shape of each shrub within a grouping. The shrubs blend together visually when they are pruned by thinning the branches.

Deciduous shrubs are best if left natural looking; avoid shearing them into formal shapes unless they are used as hedges. Whether deciduous or evergreen, individual shrubs sheared into formal shapes stand isolated from one another. This look may suit fine-textured evergreens, but the bolder look of most deciduous shrubs is better suited to a more naturalistic pruning technique. When flowering shrubs are sheared, the flowers become so crowded that they are seen as a mass

of color rather than as separate colorful blossoms with appealing shapes and outlines.

Correctly pruned shrubs look as if they have not been pruned at all. If a deciduous shrub looks as if it obviously has been pruned, probably too much has been done to it. If there is no reason for a pruning cut, don't make it. Not all plants need pruning either. Slow growers and shrubs with a well-proportioned framework are nearly trouble-free.

PRUNING GOALS

Shrubs are pruned for many reasons, but the same tools and techniques are always used.

Controlling Size

Despite their beauty and diversity, most deciduous shrubs grow beyond the space allotted for them in the landscape. For this reason alone, be prepared to prune. Common shrubs such as lilac, viburnum, and privet can grow surprisingly large, sometimes reaching 20 feet tall when mature. Few shrub species sold in nurseries will remain under 3 feet tall. Dwarf and compact-growing cultivars stay more in scale with the home landscape, but still require pruning to control size in many garden locations.

Some shrubs grow quickly, others slowly. Choose the right shrub for the space or reserve enough space to accommodate the shrub as it grows—and there will be no need for concern about growth rate. Unfortunately, availability, price, and flowering effect—not mature size—are usually the reasons for selecting particular shrubs. Consequently, large-growing shrubs often end up in small spaces. Most homeowners—and even many landscapers—are concerned that a new planting not look sparse, so they plant shrubs close together. In the space of several years, the shrubs begin to crowd each other. In this case it is better to remove or transplant every other shrub rather than prune them all severely year after year.

Only minimal pruning will be needed if shrubs are spaced so that their branches mingle slightly when they reach their mature size. Where space is limited, however, fast-growing shrubs need annual pruning. Slow growers, which make considerably fewer demands on your time, may not need yearly attention.

When allotted sufficient space at planting, slow-growing shrubs and shrubs with a naturally well-proportioned framework, such as this Kerria japonica, need little or no pruning.

Top: Without marring its beauty, appropriate pruning techniques can prevent this weigela from blocking the stairs. Bottom: When unproductive older branches are regularly removed, as with this bridal-wreath, the vigorous new growth puts on a stunning floral show. Right: Regular removal of older, brown-barked branches ensures that this red-osier dogwood will bear many young stems with red bark.

Increasing Flowering

Pruning increases flowering by encouraging new wood to form and by removing older, less-productive branches. Most deciduous flowering shrubs have multiple stems and send up new growth from the ground. Soon after these shoots develop into branches, they reach their flower-bearing prime. With age they grow less energetically. Keep flowering shrubs in a vigorous condition indefinitely by constantly removing old stems.

In the late summer, when growth begins to slow and sugars accumulate in woody branches, most deciduous flowering shrubs set flower buds for the following year. The more sugars accumulate, the more flower buds are set. Severe pruning in late winter or spring may remove so much growth that all the plant's energy goes into producing stems and leaves, with little energy left to create flower buds for the following season. Heavy pruning in late summer removes many of the flower buds that have just been set, resulting in a poor floral show the next year.

Although deciduous shrubs can renew themselves even when large quantities of old wood are removed, it is best to leave some mature flowering wood. For the showiest flower display, prune a little each year instead of waiting for the shrub to grow into a tangled mass that must be cut back severely. Thin regularly to renew the shrub, always maintaining a healthy stand of prime branches for a lively show of flowers.

Encouraging Colorful Bark

Some deciduous shrubs have attractive gray, green, red, or yellow twigs that become darker and turn brown as they age. Encourage showy new growth by thinning the oldest and darkest wood. Shrubs with vividly colored stems such as the red-osier dogwood need regular removal of old, dull-barked branches to be their most colorful.

Other shrubs such as oak-leaved hydrangea bear interesting flaking or exfoliating bark on older wood. In this case the pruning goal is just the opposite. Maximize the exfoliating effect by retaining mature branches and remove some lower branches to reveal the attractive stems.

Maintaining Shape

Try to use natural forms of shrubs to fulfill specific functions in the landscape. For example, stiffly upright shrubs can serve as space dividers, a hedge, or a living wall. Low, horizontally spreading shrubs can cascade over a bank or wall, or cover the ground. Rounded shrubs make a good background for most landscape plantings.

To enhance and maintain the inherent form, it is important to learn to prune properly and to respect the natural branching habit of the shrub. If pruning alters the shape of a shrub, the entire landscape design could be affected. Thoughtful pruning will emphasize the natural branching pattern of each species. Most shrubs have a rounded and upright, but gradually spreading, form and are easy to prune.

Shrubs like forsythia (*Forsythia* × *intermedia*) are upright when young but their branches gradually relax and cascade softly with age. Shrubby dogwoods with many small twigs give a delicate, fine-textured winter effect when massed. The horizontally spreading but somewhat stiff branches of the double file viburnum (*Viburnum plicatum tomentosum*) make a strong, bold showing in the shrub border. Dwarf winged euonymus (*Euonymus alata* 'Compacta'), with its distinct, upright, vase-shaped branching, grows so slowly that it seldom needs pruning.

Although an exceptionally handsome or unique shrub is often planted alone as a specimen, landscape plants are generally blended together in screens or borders, or used as backdrops or space definers. Separate, individual plantings cannot fill these functions.

Rejuvenating Shrubs

Neglected and overgrown shrubs with many crowded branches look unkempt, flower poorly, and are candidates for disease or insect attack. Severe pruning reshapes the plant and encourages vigorous new growth with increased vigor and more abundant flowering (see pages 48 to 49 for instructions on rejuvenating shrubs).

PRUNING TECHNIQUES FOR DECIDUOUS SHRUBS

Before pruning a shrub, consider its mature height, natural branching characteristics, and distinctive shape. Proper thinning maintains that shape regardless of the age or size of the shrub. Thinning also allows light to penetrate a shrub mass and create interesting patterns.

Pruning Deciduous Shrubs

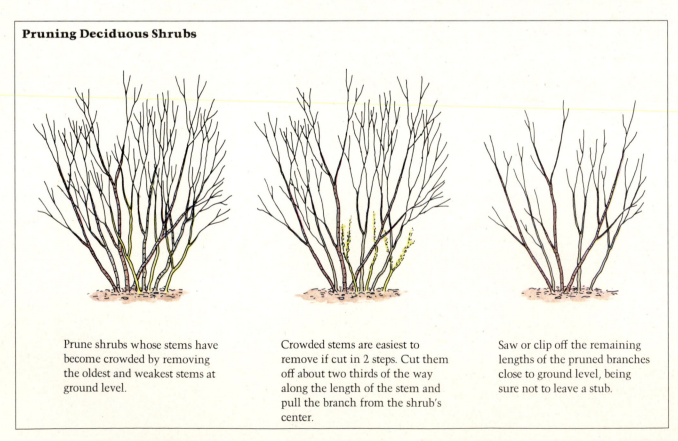

Prune shrubs whose stems have become crowded by removing the oldest and weakest stems at ground level.

Crowded stems are easiest to remove if cut in 2 steps. Cut them off about two thirds of the way along the length of the stem and pull the branch from the shrub's center.

Saw or clip off the remaining lengths of the pruned branches close to ground level, being sure not to leave a stub.

Left: This bridal-wreath has not been pruned for years and is a tangle of old and weak branches. Right: Corrective pruning with lopping shears removes the oldest and weakest branches at their bases and encourages strong new growth.

Left: Crowding the gate, this winged euonymus has outgrown its landscape space and is in need of major pruning. Right: Thinning the euonymus with hand shears removes a huge pile of twigs and branches, but the plant keeps its natural shape—only its reduced size indicates it has been pruned.

Routine Pruning

When properly pruned, deciduous shrubs consist of stems of various heights and ages, which arise directly from the ground. Removing some of the oldest stems each year or two continually makes room for new shoots to emerge. Meanwhile the remaining stems, benefitting from increased exposure to sunlight, grow and bloom more vigorously. This type of pruning gradually renews a shrub before it becomes so crowded with old stems that drastic measures are needed to improve it.

Use long-handled loppers to remove stems at or near ground level. Small curved pruning saws may be needed if the stems are larger than 1 inch in diameter or very woody. Remove one fifth to one third of the oldest, tallest, and darkest branches. Cut the branch in two steps. Begin by making a heading cut that leaves a stub about one third of the former length. After pulling out the cut branch from the mass of branches, prune the stub as close as possible to the ground. The stem is easier to remove if pruned in two steps rather than cutting the entire stem to the ground at once. Do not leave long stubs since these rarely produce satisfactory new growth. More often, the stubs die back to the ground.

Reducing Size

Thinning cuts are used to greatly reduce the size of a shrub without changing its natural branching structure. Prune a main branch back to a lateral branch with loppers or hand pruners. Cut the branch off where it forms a Y with the side branch, being careful not to leave a stub. The lateral branch should be at least two thirds the diameter of the main branch so that apical dominance and natural growth habit are maintained. Thinning cuts mimic and accelerate nature's way of shedding old, dead, and dying branches.

Pruning to the Proper Bud

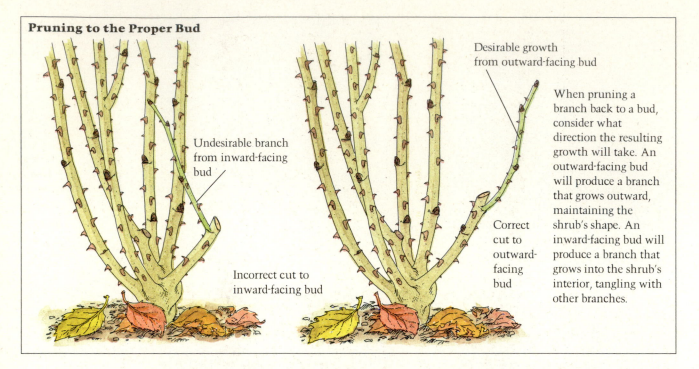

Undesirable branch from inward-facing bud

Incorrect cut to inward-facing bud

Desirable growth from outward-facing bud

Correct cut to outward-facing bud

When pruning a branch back to a bud, consider what direction the resulting growth will take. An outward-facing bud will produce a branch that grows outward, maintaining the shrub's shape. An inward-facing bud will produce a branch that grows into the shrub's interior, tangling with other branches.

Don't head branches to reduce shrub height. Heading—that is, cutting individual branches off above or below a bud or at a small-diameter lateral branch—causes many vigorously growing stems to arise directly below the cut. This can produce an unnatural flat-topped shape and crossed branches. Along with masking the branching characteristics, this type of pruning doesn't reduce the size of the shrub for long. The new growth arises quickly, soon growing beyond the pruning point. As a result of heading, a shrub actually increases gradually in height. This happens because a heading cut goes only partway into the previous season's growth, allowing the shrub to slowly grow larger. Since few, if any, new shoots will arise from the base of the shrub, the existing branches become older and less productive, and the shrub gradually declines in vigor. The dense growth at the top of the plant also reduces light penetration and slows interior growth, often leaving the inside of the shrub bare and full of dead twigs.

Corrective Pruning

Occasionally branches cross and rub, a common occurrence when one branch grows too tall. The sheer weight of the overgrown branch forces it to sag down onto a branch below. Remove the heavy branch with loppers or hand pruners and allow a younger, more upright stem to take its place.

When branches are headed rather than thinned, new growth will often originate from an inward-facing bud. The resulting branch heads into the center of the shrub, disrupts the natural growth pattern, and rubs against other branches. It's best to cut such a branch off at its origin even if it leaves an apparent hole in the foliage; new growth will soon fill in.

REJUVENATING OVERGROWN AND NEGLECTED SHRUBS

Overgrown shrubs with crowded branches or weak or misshapen stems due to previous bad pruning can be rejuvenated. There are two methods: The shrub can be gradually renewed over a period of three years or it can be drastically pruned all at once. Although the first method takes longer to produce a re-shaped plant, some shrubs respond better when gradually renewed. Drastic rejuvenation creates a temporary eyesore, but the goal is achieved more quickly than with gradual renewal.

In gradual renewal all existing branches are removed during a three- to five-year period, thus encouraging new wood to replace the old. Begin by cutting one fifth to one third of the oldest and longest stems at the ground, using loppers or a saw. In following years remove another fraction of the oldest stems until none of the original stems remains after three to five years. It may be necessary to thin

This grandiflora rose has been allowed to grow too tall and has numerous weak branches.

Lopping shears are used to remove the oldest branches at their bases. The remaining branches are then shortened to outward-facing buds.

Much reduced in size, but left with its healthiest branches, the rosebush will grow and bloom with renewed vigor.

remaining branches to restore a balanced shape to the shrub until all old growth is gone.

Some shrubs respond amazingly well when their stems or trunks are cut off at ground level all at once. Shrubs that are declining or suffering from repeated heading often respond to this shock treatment, and it is the fastest way to rejuvenate them. Numerous new shoots soon arise from the ground; select the strongest and most vigorous shoots, thinning the smallest and weakest stems. Do this extensive pruning late in the dormant season before new growth begins.

This method works well with upright shrubs such as lilac or forsythia and with spreading, horizontally branched shrubs such as cotoneaster. When their stems become too woody, cut them to the ground and new shoots will soon take the place of the old branches.

PRUNING LARGE, OVERGROWN SHRUBS INTO SMALL TREES

With careful pruning, a gangly, overgrown shrub can be transformed into a picturesque small tree. Among the best shrubs for sculpting into an artistic feature or focal point are flowering crab apple, flowering plum, viburnums such as blackhaw, gray-stem dogwood, magnolia, and winged euonymus. Others that are suitable include bottlebrush, witch hazel, and common lilac.

Begin by selecting several stems to serve as multiple trunks and remove all others. Cut off all lateral branches below the point selected for the tree canopy—usually about 4 to 6 feet above the ground, or higher if desired. Continue to remove new shoots that emerge from the base and below the canopy until the trunks grow large enough to discourage resprouting. Thin the tree canopy as needed.

WHAT TIME OF YEAR TO PRUNE

As with other woody plants, late in the dormant season just before growth begins is usually the best time to prune. At this time, stored food reserves are least affected and cuts close over most rapidly. Without a cloak of foliage on the shrub, it is easy to observe the structure of the plant and determine which branches to thin.

Right: This butterfly bush blooms in late summer on growth formed during the current season; spring pruning stimulates new growth and results in more flowers.
Below: Pruned with hand shears or loppers and not with hedge shears, this forsythia takes on a graceful shape that best displays the yellow flowers.

What about the flowers? Pruning spring-flowering shrubs in the late dormant season removes some of the flower buds set during the previous season. When pruning is restricted to a light annual thinning, however, losses are minimal; don't wait until a major pruning task is necessary because it will dramatically reduce the flower display. Although

it is possible to prune immediately after flowering, most shrubs bloom in spring—a busy time when many other tasks must be attended to in the garden. Pruning during the dormant season allows you to spread gardening activities throughout the year.

A small group of shrubs—including abelia, butterfly bush, bluebeard, hydrangea, roses, and some spirea—bloom in mid- or late summer on new wood produced in the spring and early summer. These must be pruned in the late dormant season to encourage new growth with flower buds. Pruning after growth begins only removes the flower buds.

By understanding how plants respond to pruning and by using good judgment, it is possible to prune lightly almost any time of the year without harming the plant. The vigor of many flowering shrubs won't suffer if pruned just after flowering, especially if leaves have not fully developed. Limit late-summer pruning, however, because it stimulates the growth of new shoots, which can be injured by cold winter temperatures.

PRUNING TECHNIQUES FOR HEDGES

Most hedges are formal; they are sheared into flat-sided shapes to form low or tall walls. Such hedges, which serve as living fences or privacy screens in small spaces, look neat if kept regularly trimmed. Informal hedges, maintained with loppers or handheld pruners, have a looser, more natural shape than formal hedges. It may seem to be more work to prune an informal hedge compared to shearing a formal one, but it really isn't because the informal hedge needs to be pruned less often. Expect to dedicate more space to an informal hedge to accommodate the natural branching patterns.

At planting time, decide whether you want a formal or informal hedge. A formal hedge must be pruned to a definite size and shaped at least once, and usually two or more times, each growing season. Allow shrubs in an informal hedge to grow normally, but thin a portion of the oldest branches and stems annually to maintain a uniform rate of growth and to limit height and spread.

An informal hedge made of deciduous flowering shrubs offers the double benefit of striking foliage and a massive array of flowers. Although flowering shrubs can also be used for

Starting a Hedge

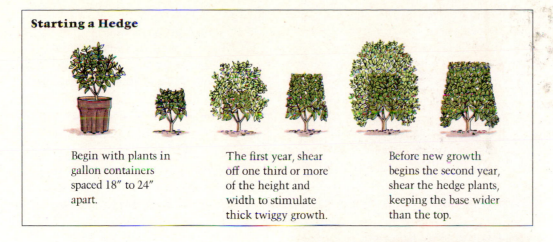

Begin with plants in gallon containers spaced 18″ to 24″ apart.

The first year, shear off one third or more of the height and width to stimulate thick twiggy growth.

Before new growth begins the second year, shear the hedge plants, keeping the base wider than the top.

formal hedges, shearing must be carefully timed so that flower buds aren't removed. Wait until just after flowering to shear each year. If the hedge needs another shearing, be certain it is early enough in the summer before next season's flower buds are set. If timing isn't careful, the result is a patchwork of green foliage and bright blossoms instead of a uniform display.

Creating a Formal Hedge

Start a formal deciduous hedge by planting one- or two-year-old shrubs in a row, 1 to 2 feet apart. Cut the shrubs back to 2 or 3 inches above the ground. Don't be afraid to take this step; it prevents the hedge from becoming leggy. No more pruning is needed the first year.

For a new hedge begun with older, taller shrubs, cut back about one third the height and width. This encourages many thick, twiggy stems to grow from the ends of the stubs. Do not prune again the first year unless the new growth becomes unusually tall.

The most important step in starting a formal hedge occurs during the second year when the hedge is first shaped with hedge shears. Before new growth begins in spring level the sides and top, keeping the base of the hedge wider than the top. The goal is to establish a narrow pyramid or inverted V. For example, a well-proportioned hedge 5 feet tall can be 2½ feet wide at the base and 1 foot wide at the top. Although often overlooked, this tapering is important because it prevents the top from shading the bottom and causing the lower part of the hedge to lose its foliage. Shear again after the first flush of growth; cut about halfway through the pliable new stems before they mature and harden. Fast-growing shrubs like privet may need a third-shearing.

To create a formal effect, nonflowering deciduous shrubs can be sheared with hedge shears into neat walls of green foliage.

In the third year continue to establish the pattern and shape of a formal hedge. Before the leaves emerge in spring or just after the first flush of growth, level the top and shear the sides so they taper from a wide base to a narrower top. Be certain this task is completed early enough in spring so that new growth covers the bare stubs.

Stretch a line between temporary posts at each end of the hedge to help keep cuts straight. The top can be flat, slightly rounded, or pointed. The taller the hedge, the more attention must be paid to maintaining proper shape and taper. If the top becomes as wide or wider than the base, it will shade the branches below and produce thin, weak growth.

Some hedges require only one shearing each year; others may need several starting early in June, and then again in mid-July and early September. Climate and rate of growth will influence this schedule.

After the hedge reaches the desired height, shear just above the start of the previous year's growth. These short intervals of growth increase the height of the hedge gradually year after year. If the hedge eventually grows too tall, rejuvenate it by cutting it to the ground as described previously (see pages 48 and 49).

Planting and Pruning an Informal Hedge

Start an informal hedge by planting shrubs 3 to 6 feet apart. Use the wider spacing for a taller hedge or for naturally large-growing plants. This allows the shrubs to spread gracefully as they grow. With one- or two-year-old plants, cut back all branches to within 2 to 3 inches of the ground to promote denseness. The only pruning required during the next few years is to thin and remove dead, broken, and diseased limbs.

For an informal hedge begun with larger plants, do not cut back at planting time. Allow the shrubs to grow naturally, pruning only wayward or broken branches.

Beginning the second year and continuing every year after, thin some of the branches arising from the base. Cut to the ground one fifth to one quarter of the tallest, oldest, and largest stems. This keeps an informal hedge youthful and vigorous for years. Use long-handled loppers or hand pruners, not hedge shears. Make the cuts as close to the ground as possible.

Espalier

A sunny, blank wall or a narrow garden is an ideal location for an espaliered shrub. The practice of training fruit trees against warm south-facing walls was begun centuries ago. For extra frost protection the plant was sometimes attached to a hollow wall in which fires would be lit.

Almost any deciduous or evergreen tree or shrub with flexible branches—for example, forsythia, cotoneaster, viburnum, yew, or pyracantha—can be espaliered. Avoid woody plants with stiff, rigid, upright growth habits.

Begin by establishing a framework of lattice, wires, hooks, or supports upon which to tie shrubs or trees. Use special hooks or rust-resistant nails for brick or masonry walls. On wood surfaces leave about 6 inches between the plant and wall for air movement.

Apple trees and crab apples are especially good to espalier. Stretch horizontal wires 18 inches apart along a wall. Plant a bare-root, one-year-old whip and head the top just below the bottom wire. From the emerging new shoots, select one to grow up to the next wire 18 inches above. Pick two side shoots to grow along the wire in each direction and tie them on. Rub off all other growth on the trunk and pinch shoots on the branches to keep them short.

During the first or second season, cut the main stem off just below the second wire from the bottom. This will initiate another set of buds, two of which should be kept for side branches and one for the trunk extension. Train these as for the first set. To make fruiting spurs on apples, cut back the lateral branches on the horizontal limbs to three buds.

Continue training until three wires, or more if desired, are covered with branches. When the tree reaches the top wire, eliminate the trunk extension by heading it, and retain the two side branches.

For extra convenience, make a wood or wire trellis and attach it to a wall with hinges at the base and hooks on top. When painting the wall, unhook the top of the trellis and carefully lean the espaliered plant, trellis and all, away from the building until the paint is dry.

Regular pruning is necessary during the growing season to restrict plants to a single flat plane. Again be sure to use thinning cuts rather than heading cuts.

Pruning Vines

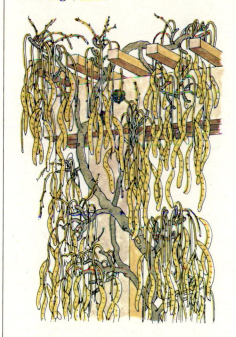

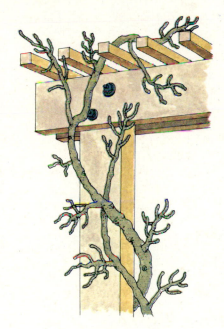

Chinese wisteria (*Wisteria sinensis*) needs pruning in late winter before new growth begins. Remove the tangle of flower stems and pods and any crowded or crossed side branches.

Leave only the flowering spurs and the permanent framework of the vine—the desirable main stems and smaller branches.

Shorten the flowering spurs to a half-dozen or so buds to encourage larger flowers and separate, free-hanging clusters.

Rejuvenating an Overgrown And Neglected Hedge

To rejuvenate an old sheared formal hedge, cut back around 8 inches lower than the desired height and width. To restore the thick surface growth, shear the new shoots as they arise. An informal hedge may be rejuvenated by gradual renewal or by cutting it all the way to the ground as described on pages 48 and 49.

PRUNING VINES

Deciduous vines, like shrubs, benefit from pruning. Occasionally it is necessary to limit growth, improve flowering, or remove deadwood or weak stems and branches. Vines respond like other landscape plants to pruning. Always prune back to a lateral branch, twig, or bud and do not leave a stub. Cut dead, weak, and thin branches back to healthy, vigorous stems. Annual thinning encourages new growth and continual rejuvenation. When stems grow too crowded, cut back some of them to the ground.

Most vines respond best to pruning in the late dormant season, before spring growth begins. Prune early-spring flowering vines after blooming to encourage maximum bud set on new growth. Every year in early spring cut back to 6 to 8 inches aboveground vines that flower on new wood—for example, many types of clematis.

Fast-growing vines require yearly pruning. Some particularly vigorous vines will overwhelm a garden, develop a barren woody trunk, or become overcrowded if not kept in check. Cut back these vigorous growers severely to induce new growth close to the ground. This is not harmful as long as it is done before spring growth begins. Contain fast-spreading vines such as Boston ivy by cutting stems to the ground, heading to a bud, or thinning to a lateral.

When a vine becomes unmanageable from lack of yearly pruning, cut it to the ground and let it start over. When the new stems appear, select the most desirable and remove the rest. Pinch the tips of climbing stems to slow their upward growth temporarily.

Berberis thunbergii (Japanese barberry)

Cornus alba (Tartarian dogwood)

DECIDUOUS SHRUB PRUNING ENCYCLOPEDIA

This encyclopedia describes the best pruning methods for many of the deciduous shrubs that are commonly grown in home gardens. The shrubs are listed alphabetically by botanical name. If you know only the common name of a particular shrub, refer to the index to determine its botanical name.

Acer palmatum
Japanese maple, cut-leaf maple

Often used as a specimen shrub, this small tree is available in cultivars that seldom grow more than 10 feet tall. 'Burgundy Lace', one of the most common cultivars, has finely cut, reddish leaves.

How to prune Maintain the umbrellalike shape. Remove crossing branches, thin excessive inside growth, and train some branches upward to promote a layered effect.

When to prune Late dormant season.

Berberis thunbergii
Japanese barberry

This thorny shrub grows about 5 feet tall and wide.

How to prune Although barberry can be sheared into a formal hedge, it's better to let it grow naturally. Thin at the base to maintain size and shape. Rejuvenate by removing old wood at the ground.

When to prune Late dormant season for major cuts; anytime for touch-up pruning.

Buddleia species
Butterfly bush, orange-eye buddleia, summer lilac

These fast-growing shrubs can grow to between 7 and 15 feet tall. They die to the ground in cold-winter areas, but are semievergreen in mild-winter climates.

How to prune Cut to the ground each year if frost doesn't kill top portions. Flowers on new growth.

When to prune Late dormant season.

Calycanthus species
Allspice, pineapple shrub, spicebush, strawberry shrub, sweet shrub

Growing to about 10 feet tall and 7 feet wide, these shrubs have aromatic foliage. They develop several stems close to the ground.

How to prune Thin to keep small and to shape.

When to prune Late dormant season.

Caryopteris × clandonensis
Hybrid bluebeard, blue mist

This shrub does not grow more than 4 feet tall. It can be treated as a perennial in cold-winter areas where it usually dies back to the ground each year. Intense blue flowers bloom in late summer and fall on new growth.

How to prune When not killed back naturally, cut to within a few inches of the ground to force maximum new growth.

When to prune Late dormant season.

Chaenomeles species
Flowering quince

One of the earliest spring-flowering shrubs, flowering quince grows around 6 feet tall and wide. Roselike flowers are borne on wood that is one year old and older.

How to prune Start training when young by thinning a few branches at the ground every year. Thin the tangled center of an older neglected shrub by removing the oldest stems at the ground.

When to prune Dormant season or after flowering.

Cornus alba
Tartarian dogwood

See *Cornus sericea*

Cornus sericea (Cornus stolonifera)
Red-osier dogwood, red-twig dogwood

These vase-shaped shrubs, growing about 10 feet tall and wide, have attractive bright red stems.

Cotoneaster horizontalis (rock spray cotoneaster)

Euonymus alata (winged euonymus)

Forsythia × intermedia (border forsythia)

How to prune Thin one third of the oldest stems at the base every year to promote new growth with brightly colored bark.

When to prune Late dormant season.

Corylus avellana
European filbert,
European hazel

This shrub grows 10 to 15 feet tall and as wide. The cultivar 'Contorta' has twisted corkscrew branches.

How to prune This plant can be trained as a small tree or multitrunked shrub. For a single trunk select the strongest stem when young and remove suckers as they appear. If growing it as a shrub, thin occasionally.

When to prune Dormant season.

Cotoneaster species
Cotoneaster

Among the many forms of cotoneaster are deciduous and evergreen shrubs ranging in height from several inches to 20 feet tall.

How to prune Remove dead wood from low growers and thin annually. Since old wood readily resprouts, thin to the ground. Don't shear because branch stubs remain unattractive for some time. Tall growers look best if pruned to emphasize the natural fountainlike shape. Since all species are susceptible to fire blight, remove scorched-looking dead branches and cut well into the healthy wood.

When to prune Late dormant season.

Cytisus species (also Genista and Spartium)
Broom

Brooms include members of three different genera: *Cytisus*, *Genista*, and *Spartium*. Ranging in size from small garden miniatures to spreading shrubs, they can be deciduous or evergreen. Most of these flowering plants have green stems.

How to prune Cut back stems by one third, taking care not to cut into older, leafless wood because old stems rarely resprout. For the same reason rejuvenating old twiggy specimens is difficult.

When to prune After flowering.

Deutzia scabra
Deutzia, fuzzy deutzia

This spring-flowering shrub, can reach 10 feet tall; becomes scraggly without pruning.

How to prune Thin annually to keep it neat and compact. If necessary cut to the ground every five years or so to rejuvenate.

When to prune After flowering.

Euonymus alata
Winged euonymus,
winged spindle tree

This popular shrub makes a formal or informal hedge, as well as a dramatic specimen growing 10 feet tall and wide.

How to prune Little pruning is required. Thin selectively every other year for an informal plant or shear into a formal hedge.

When to prune Late dormant season.

Exochorda racemosa
Pearlbush

Slow-growing, this vase-shaped flowering shrub eventually reaches about 12 feet tall and wide.

How to prune Since pearlbush can become leggy, selectively thin branches to the ground. To rejuvenate remove one third of the oldest wood to the ground each year for three years.

When to prune After flowering or during dormancy.

Forsythia × intermedia
Border forsythia

Fast-growing with arching branches, this spring-flowering shrub reaches 6 feet.

How to prune Once mature, thin some of the oldest wood at the base every year. If suckers become excessive, cut most of them to the ground but leave some to replace the stems that have been removed. To reduce size, thin the tallest branches.

When to prune Dormant season until after flowering.

Hydrangea macrophylla (bigleaf hydrangea)

Kerria japonica (Japanese rose)

Fuchsia × hybrida
Fuchsia

This flowering shrub is deciduous in cold climates and semievergreen to evergreen in mild-winter areas. It can be trained as a shrub or standard.

How to prune Each year remove most of the previous season's growth. Thin standards periodically to prevent tangling.

When to prune After first frost and before spring growth where plant is deciduous; late dormant season where plant retains leaves.

Hamamelis species
Witch hazel

Some species of witch hazel are wide-spreading and others are vase-shaped. Most can grow 30 feet tall, but usually remain about 15 feet tall.

How to prune *Hamamelis mollis* (Chinese witch hazel) doesn't respond well to pruning. For other species, thin the most vigorous growth when the plant reaches the desired height. Witch hazel can be trained into a small tree with

a single trunk by selecting the strongest stem when young. Pinch side growth and remove suckers until the trunk reaches the desired height. Then remove branches on the trunk and shape the crown.

When to prune Before or after flowering; branches removed in winter can be forced into bloom indoors.

Hydrangea macrophylla
Bigleaf hydrangea, French hydrangea, hortensia

This midsummer flowering shrub blooms on buds formed the previous season. It can reach 12 feet tall but 5 to 8 feet is more common.

How to prune When neglected, hydrangea tends to grow thin and woody with just an umbrella of foliage above the stems. Cut back stems that have flowered to about 2 feet from the ground. Rejuvenate specimens that failed to flower by cutting back every cane in a similar manner.

When to prune As soon as blooms have faded.

Hydrangea paniculata 'Grandiflora'
Panicle hydrangea, peegee hydrangea

This vigorous shrub, which blooms in summer on new growth, can reach up to 30 feet tall if trained as a tree.

How to prune If the shrub becomes overgrown, thin three or four main branches about 2 feet from the ground. To maintain as a hedge, clip the fastest growing shoots frequently. For a tree, thin laterals and suckers annually to maintain several trunks.

When to prune Late dormant season.

Ilex (deciduous species)
Holly, black-alder, possumhaw, yaupon, winterberry

Although most hollies are evergreen, several deciduous species that grow 5 to 30 feet tall are notable landscape plants.

How to prune Thin old growth to rejuvenate.

When to prune Late dormant season.

Kerria japonica
Japanese rose, kerria

This spring-flowering shrub grows to about 8 feet tall with an open form. Twigs are bright green all year.

How to prune Because flowers appear on the previous year's growth, cut canes that have flowered or are weak to the ground. New stems have the best green color.

When to prune After flowering.

Kolkwitzia amabilis
Beautybush

Growing in an arching or vase shape to 10 or 12 feet tall, beautybush flowers on the previous season's growth.

How to prune Cut one quarter to one third of the oldest canes to the ground each year to stimulate new growth. To prune a neglected specimen, cut it to the ground.

When to prune After flowering.

Magnolia stellata (star magnolia)

Rhododendron hybrid (Exbury azalea)

Philadelphus coronarius (mock orange)

Ligustrum (deciduous species)
Privet

Privet is probably the most commonly used deciduous hedge plant. It withstands heavy shearing but can also be allowed to grow naturally. Height depends on species.

How to prune Shear to maintain a formal hedge. Thin at base as needed to maintain an informal shrub or hedge.

When to prune Late dormant season for shearing; growing season for touch-up.

Lonicera species
Bush honeysuckle

Several species of honeysuckle are useful landscape shrubs. *L. nitida* forms a neat 4- to 6-foot-tall shrub or can be sheared into a formal hedge. *L. tatarica* is a 9-foot-tall vase, and *L. fragrantissima*, becoming a rounded mass up to 9 feet tall and wide, makes useful informal hedges.

How to prune Thin branches at the ground to rejuvenate and control size.

When to prune Late dormant season.

Magnolia × soulangiana
Saucer magnolia

This multitrunked magnolia can reach 30 feet tall. Magnolias are susceptible to diseases that can infect the wood through large wounds.

How to prune Prune lower branches to reveal multiple trunks. Needs little pruning.

When to prune Late dormant season or after flowering.

Magnolia stellata
Star magnolia

This bushy magnolia forms a dense shrub or small tree 15 feet or taller.

How to prune It needs very little pruning. Eliminate poorly placed branches when they are small. Magnolias are susceptible to diseases that can infect the wood through large wounds.

When to prune Late dormant season is best; it can also be pruned after flowering.

Philadelphus coronarius
Sweet mock orange, mock orange

Mock orange is a vase-shaped, fragrant-flowering shrub growing to 10 feet tall.

How to prune Since it flowers on the previous year's growth, prune to promote strong new growth for the best floral display. Cut one third to one quarter of the oldest canes to the ground annually.

When to prune After flowering or late dormant season.

Prunus × cistena
Purple-leaf sand cherry

A small, rapidly growing shrub reaching 8 to 10 feet tall, this plant has intense reddish purple foliage that holds its color all summer.

How to prune Thin old or crowded canes at the base annually.

When to prune After flowering.

Prunus glandulosa
Dwarf flowering almond

This spring-blooming shrub flowers on one-year-old wood. It grows to a height and width of 5 feet.

How to prune Cut back hard to stimulate new growth.

When to prune Immediately after blooming.

Rhododendron species and cultivars
Deciduous azaleas

Deciduous azaleas include the many species native to North America and Asia and their hybrids, including cultivars of the Exbury, Mollis, and Knap Hill groups.

How to prune Little pruning is needed except to remove deadwood and spent flower trusses. Large plants may be thinned dramatically to reduce their size or cut back by one third each year for 3 years.

When to prune Late dormant season.

Spiraea × vanhouttei (bridal wreath)

Rosa hybrid (climbing polyantha rose)

Viburnum sargentii, right, and *V. plicatum*, left (viburnum)

Rosa species and cultivars
Rose

Whether hybrid teas, grandifloras, floribundas, or climbers, all roses need extensive pruning to promote the best flowering.

How to prune   Roses may be pruned lightly or cut almost to the ground every year, depending upon the gardener's preference. The usual practice is to remove about one third of the previous season's growth. For hybrid bush types, remove all deadwood and cut back old canes to develop an attractive open framework; this encourages new growth, which flowers the same season. Remove at the base canes that produced only weak growth. Make cuts at a 45-degree angle about ¼ inch above a leaf bud. Be sure the center of the cut canes is creamy-white or light green; brown-centered canes are injured and should be cut further into healthy wood.

When cutting flowers for display, be sure to leave enough foliage behind to nourish the plant. Leave at least two five-leaflet leaves on the remaining branch and cut to an outward-facing leaf.

Climbing roses should not be heavily pruned for several years; remove dead or weak canes and spent flowers. The pruning goal after climbers are established is to promote lateral stems that produce the flowers. Remove older and less productive canes each year. On the remaining canes cut all the side branches that flowered during the previous season to two or three buds.

Ramblers are climbing roses that bloom prolifically in early summer on one-year-old wood. After flowering many new canes grow from the base of the plant. When blooming has finished, remove the canes that flowered and train the new ones to a trellis or fence.

When to prune   Late dormant season for most types of roses; after flowering for ramblers.

Spiraea species
Bridal wreath, spirea

Most spireas bloom in spring on the previous season's wood. A few others flower in summer on new wood; these include *S. albiflora*, *S. bullata*, *S. × bumalda*, *S. japonica*, and *S. × margaritae*.

How to prune   Thin annually to promote vigorous growth and flowering. Rejuvenate thick clumps by removing old canes at the ground.

When to prune   Dormant season; spring-flowering species that bloom on old wood can be pruned after flowering.

Syringa vulgaris
Common lilac

These multistemmed shrubs can grow as tall as 15 to 20 feet. If not well-pruned, flowers grow only at the top.

How to prune   Leave lilacs alone for the first few years except to remove suckers. Each year thereafter, remove one third of the oldest stems. Rejuvenate neglected plants by cutting back one third each year for 3 years or cut completely to the ground. Remove faded flower heads to increase flowering.

When to prune   Dormant season or after flowering.

Viburnum species
Viburnum, cranberry bush, European cranberry

There are numerous viburnum species, most of which grow 12 to 15 feet tall. They are spring-flowering shrubs with decorative fall berries.

How to prune   Need little pruning. Thin oldest wood to the ground periodically. To train as a single- or multiple-trunk tree, choose the most likely stems when young and thin side shoots until the trunk reaches the desired height.

When to prune   Late dormant season.

Weigela hybrids
Weigela

These spring-flowering shrubs bloom on one-year-old wood. Older varieties grow large, but cultivars mature at 10 feet.

How to prune   Frequent pruning will keep weigela to almost any size. Thin branches that have flowered to a side branch or the ground. Remove oldest wood annually.

When to prune   After flowering.

Campsis radicans (trumpet creeper)

Bougainvillea species (paper flower)

VINE PRUNING ENCYCLOPEDIA

This encyclopedia describes the best pruning methods for many of the deciduous and evergreen vines that are commonly grown in home gardens. The vines are listed alphabetically by botanical name. If you know only the common name for a particular vine, refer to the index to determine its botanical name.

Actinidia chinensis
Kiwi berry, Chinese gooseberry

This vigorous deciduous vine, which blooms and fruits on old wood, needs regular pruning.

How to prune Kiwi can be pruned heavily. Remove old wood on established plants annually to encourage new shoots. Cut above strong buds that point in the desired direction.

When to prune When the buds begin to grow.

Akebia quinata
Five-leaf akebia

Deciduous in cold climates and semievergreen to evergreen in mild-winter areas, this vigorous vine can grow 15 feet in a single year. It matures at 30 feet or more.

How to prune Thin yearly after flowering to control the size and shape. If the vine becomes overgrown, cut it to the ground to rejuvenate.

When to prune Dormant season or after flowering.

Bignonia capreolata (also Anisostichus capreolatus, Campsis capreolata, and Doxantha capreolata)
Scarlet trumpet vine, trumpet flower, cross vine, quarter vine

This evergreen vine bears trumpet-shaped flowers on new wood.

How to prune Cut off suckers as soon as they appear. Remove spent flowering shoots to encourage new growth.

When to prune Dormant season.

Bougainvillea species
Paper flower, bougainvillea

This vigorous tropical evergreen vine requires regular pruning to keep it within bounds.

How to prune Remove old, weak-blooming shoots and cut laterals back to two buds for profuse flowering. Remove frost-damaged stems, but wait until spring when many apparently frost-killed shoots suddenly show life.

When to prune After flowering.

Campsis radicans
Trumpet creeper

This deciduous woody vine, growing to 20 feet, blooms in midsummer on new growth. A desirable ornamental in cold-winter climates, trumpet creeper can be a rampant weed in mild climates.

How to prune Eliminate the spent flower-bearing shoots each year. Pinch growing tips to promote branching. Remove suckers as they appear, especially in mild climates.

When to prune Dormant season.

Celastrus scandens
Bittersweet, climbing bittersweet, staff vine

This rampant-growing deciduous vine can choke out nearby plants if not controlled. It is grown primarily for decorative berrylike fruit which remains on the vine after leaves drop.

How to prune Remove branches with spent fruit. Pinch the tips in summer to promote branching. If a vine becomes too tangled or develops too many old branches, cut it to the ground when dormant. Dig out suckers with a spade.

When to prune Dormant season; branches bearing fruit can be pruned for display indoors.

Clematis 'Nelly Moser' (clematis)

Hydrangea anomala ssp. *petiolaris* (climbing hydrangea)

Clematis species
Clematis, virgin's bower

The many species and cultivars of clematis, most of them deciduous, require different pruning methods.

How to prune One of the few evergreen species, *C. armandii* (Armand clematis) is a rampant grower; after spring bloom prune heavily by removing excess stems. *C. × jackmanii* (Jackman clematis) flowers on new wood in summer; prune in late dormant season by cutting back to 6 to 12 inches from the ground or to the first two or three buds on a young plant. *C. lanuginosa* blooms on old wood in spring and on new wood in summer; after spring-flowering laterals have bloomed, remove them to encourage summer flowering. *C. montana* (anemone clematis) is a vigorous vine that blooms on old wood in spring; prune after flowering and train it horizontally to prevent it from becoming top-heavy; prune old, tangled vines as the buds start to grow in spring and remove all unproductive wood. *C.* 'Nelly Moser', 'Ramona', and 'Duchess of Edinburgh' are cultivars that bloom in spring and again in summer. Prune as for *C. lanuginosa*.

When to prune Late dormant season or summer, according to growth and blooming schedule.

Euonymus fortunei varieties
Wintercreeper

See *Euonymus* in evergreen shrub listing.

Gelsemium sempervirens
Evening trumpet flower, Carolina jessamine, yellow jessamine, Carolina jasmine

Growing to 20 feet, this easily managed evergreen vine with pretty yellow flowers in spring can also be used as an effective ground cover.

How to prune Remove dead and broken branches. Prune heavily as needed and then shape by shearing.

When to prune After flowering.

Hedera helix
English ivy

This is a tough, rapidly growing evergreen vine for climbing or ground cover. It can grow 100 feet.

How to prune Prune annually in spring to control growth. Vines trained in patterns on a wall may need pruning every few weeks during growth. If ground cover becomes leggy, mow or cut back with hedge shears.

When to prune Anytime; late dormant season for major rejuvenation.

Hydrangea anomala
Climbing hydrangea

This deciduous vine, which can grow to 75 feet with 3-foot-long branches, flowers in midsummer on new wood.

How to prune Once established, thin vigorously or cut back to the ground occasionally to limit growth and encourage new wood.

When to prune Late dormant season.

Ipomoea species
Morning-glory, moonflower

These include perennial and annual vines.

How to prune Cut perennial species to the ground each winter; retrain in the spring.

When to prune Dormant season.

Jasminum nudiflorum
Winter jasmine

This deciduous woody vine flowers in early spring on old wood. Regular pruning is needed to control its growth.

How to prune Remove one third of the growth each year to leave old flowering wood.

When to prune After flowering.

Lonicera japonica
Honeysuckle

Evergreen in most areas and deciduous in cold climates, this vine blooms all summer long. Quickly reaching 15 feet, the vine's rampant growth must be controlled before it climbs up and chokes nearby trees and shrubs.

Parthenocissus quinquefolia (Virginia creeper)

Wisteria sinensis (Chinese wisteria)

How to prune Every year head mature plants and thin crowded stems. Remove suckers when they appear.

When to prune Dormant season or after flowering.

Parthenocissus quinquefolia

Virginia creeper, American ivy

See *Parthenocissus tricuspidata*

Parthenocissus tricuspidata

Boston ivy

These deciduous vines—Boston ivy is semievergreen in warm-winter areas—are best on trellises or building walls. Tolerant of any amount of pruning, Virginia creeper and Boston ivy must be controlled before they choke and smother nearby trees and shrubs.

How to prune Cut off any part of the vine that is torn from its support since ruptured suction pads will not reattach themselves. Remove dead or diseased sections. To rejuvenate, cut to the ground.

When to prune Late dormant season to redirect and control growth; anytime for touch-up pruning.

Passiflora species

Passion vine

These flowering vines include evergreen, semievergreen, and deciduous species. Rampant growers, they must be controlled from an early age.

How to prune If it begins to grow out of control, cut back to the ground. Keep it sheared neatly by pruning in the spring when new growth will quickly cover the cuts.

When to prune Dormant season.

Polygonum aubertii

Silver lace vine

Evergreen in mild-winter areas and deciduous in cold-climates, this rapid-growing vine may die to the ground in severe winters. Creamy white flowers bloom in summer and early fall on new wood.

How to prune This vine can be allowed to grow nearly

unchecked during the growing season. Cut it to the ground or to one or two stems to stimulate flowering.

When to prune Late dormant season; wait until after frost danger has passed in cold-winter areas.

Solanum jasminoides

Jasmine nightshade, potato vine

Evergreen in mild-winter areas and deciduous in cold climates, this vine grows quickly to 20 feet. It blooms in summer on new wood.

How to prune Remove excess growth and cut back as needed to promote branching.

When to prune Late dormant season.

Trachelospermum jasminoides

Star jasmine

An evergreen vine that grows slowly to 15 feet, star jasmine bears fragrant flowers in spring and summer. It can also be grown as a ground cover.

How to prune If it becomes too bare or produces fewer flowers, thin old woody growth to main branches.

When to prune Late dormant season.

Wisteria floribunda and W. sinensis

Wisteria

These heavy deciduous vines are covered with fragrant flowers in spring. The vines grow rapidly to a huge size.

How to prune Let a young vine grow unpruned until it has reached the desired size. In winter thin all new growth to the second bud. In spring remove all leafless shoots as they form. Prune laterals to two or three buds, leaving the spurs, which are loaded with flower buds. In summer remove leafless shoots and shorten laterals by half. Support main branches well because they become thick and heavy as the vine branches during the year. Remove suckers on grafted varieties.

When to prune Throughout the year as described above.

Pruning Evergreen Shrubs and Trees

Evergreens, both needled and broadleaf, need special care during pruning to prevent injury to their foliage. Find out how to prune evergreens so they look natural but stay small—proper timing and tools are crucial.

Evergreen trees and shrubs, stalwart garden companions, hold their greenery the year around. Although alike in this respect, evergreens vary in many other ways. Some have fine-needled foliage or bold leaves in various shades of green. Others offer unusual cones, gleaming berries, or colorful blossoms. Although attractive in their own right, one of the greatest garden assets offered by evergreens is their ability to screen unsightly views. Both evergreen shrubs and trees can provide year-round privacy, blocking unwelcome views or viewers. They also make effective—and beautiful—windbreaks and snowfences.

Where winters are cold, evergreens are often limited by the harsh climate; there they are all the more valued for their winter greenery, a welcome contrast to bare-limbed deciduous plants. In warmer climates evergreens, particularly broadleaf kinds, abound. However, be careful not to use too many evergreen trees close to the house. In overabundance they have a somber effect, and block welcome sunshine, especially in winter.

Unfortunately, many evergreens need pruning to stay within the size and scale of most home landscapes. Properly pruned, these plants will remain handsome for decades. Despite their dependability for hiding, screening, softening, and backdropping, not all evergreens are forgiving of and responsive to pruning. It is important to know when and how to prune to achieve good results.

Both needled and broadleaf evergreens add to the year-round beauty of this garden, creating a beautiful setting in every season.

EVERGREEN SHAPES

Just as deciduous trees and shrubs have distinct shapes, so do evergreens; they can be rounded, oval, pyramidal, upright, horizontal, weeping, or irregular. The natural branching pattern of the plant dictates its shape. By respecting this inherent form when pruning it is possible to limit the size of an evergreen without changing its shape. Not only does this preserve the plant's true beauty, but it saves the expense of replacing overgrown plants.

Evergreen shrubs are often sheared into individual geometrical forms to create a formal shape and to slow the plant's growth. Altering a natural plant shape by shearing commits the gardener to spending more time and energy in maintaining the sheared form than if the natural shape had been respected. Although shearing does limit size to some extent, a sheared evergreen gradually grows larger over the years because shearing removes only part of the previous season's growth. Sheared shrubs can eventually outgrow their space, while those that are pruned by thinning can usually be kept at the desired size.

DIFFERENT KINDS OF EVERGREENS

There are three basic kinds of evergreens: needled or needleleaf, narrowleaf, and broadleaf.

Needled and Narrowleaf Evergreens

The vast majority of needled and narrowleaf evergreens aren't flowering plants, but produce naked seeds borne in woody or fleshy cones; scientists refer to them as gymnosperms, a classification containing numerous plant families. Many important landscape evergreens, such as pine, spruce, fir, and hemlock, produce their seeds in woody cones and belong to a plant grouping called conifers. The foliage on needled evergreens may be flat-sided as in fir, square as in spruce, or triangular as in pine. Other conifers, such as juniper are narrowleaved evergreens with flat needlelike leaves or scales pressed against the stem. They have fleshy cones resembling berries.

Broadleaf Evergreens

In contrast, broadleaf evergreens, such as rhododendrons, holly, boxwood, laurel, Indian hawthorn, and euonymus, bear flat leaves

similar to those of deciduous plants—except that the foliage remains green the year around. They are a diverse group of plants whose foliage may actually be fine-, medium-, or coarse-textured and come in various shapes and sizes. Broadleaf evergreens are angiosperms or flowering plants; the flowers may be showy as on rhododendrons or inconspicuous as on holly.

GROWTH PATTERNS

Most needled and broadleaf evergreens send out a single flush of growth each year in spring. After this growth matures in midsummer, the plant develops new terminal buds, which remain dormant until the following year. Needled evergreens start growing each spring from these buds initiated during the previous growing season. Pines, for example,

Top: Junipers are popular narrowleaf evergreens for home landscapes.
Bottom: Pittosporum is an evergreen that has broad, flat leaves rather than needles.

Left: On conifers the flush of new growth from terminal buds at the end of each branch is called a candle. To control the size of the plant, pinch back candles before the needles enlarge. Right: Many conifers, such as blue spruce, bear tiers of symmetrical branches that cloak the central trunk; the trees look best when lower branches are allowed to sweep the ground.

produce a single flush of growth from terminal buds on the end of every branch. This soft new growth, consisting of a flexible stem and developing bundles of needles, is called a candle. (Pines are easily recognized by their bundles of two, three, or five needles enclosed in a papery basal sheath.) Growth from the largest terminal bud becomes the new leader for that branch; smaller buds below the terminal become side branches. This pattern of growth produces the whorled branching characteristic of needled evergreens. The age of a tree or branch can be determined by counting the number of whorls of side branches; each year a new whorl of growth is added.

Some broadleaf evergreens grow in a similar manner. Rhododendrons, for example, produce a flush of succulent stems and leaves from buds located to the side of each flower bud. Dormant buds develop at the stem tips in midsummer and grow the next spring.

Most narrowleaf evergreens have a random branching pattern, not a whorled one; they grow in spurts during the spring and summer giving the appearance of continual growth. Junipers, false cypress, and arborvitae are good examples. In yews the spring growth spurt is followed by a second flush in midsummer.

Unlike deciduous shrubs, not all evergreens resprout from old wood if pruned back. This is especially true of needled evergreens. They grow primarily from buds set the previous year and have few if any latent buds. It is safe to prune back only to one- or two-year-old wood, which has existing buds, if the goal is to

stimulate new growth. Otherwise prune back a branch to where it forks into side branches. Pine and arborvitae will not rejuvenate if pruned heavily into wood that bears no obvious buds, even if that wood contains needles. Narrowleaf evergreens such as yew and juniper resprout from old wood as long as they are pruned back to growth that still contains foliage.

Some broadleaf evergreens such as azaleas, rhododendrons, pyracantha, and holly develop latent or adventitious buds. These shrubs can be cut back to old wood or just above the ground if necessary to rejuvenate them.

The branches of conifers, unlike branches of deciduous trees, fill the entire trunk from the ground to the uppermost leader. The lower branches sweeping the ground and the strong pyramidal form of many coniferous trees define their landscape beauty. The more pyramidal the tree's form and the thicker the foliage, the more important it is to retain the lower branches. Spruce and fir, which have dense whorls of branches filling a symmetrical pyramid, need their lower branches to visually anchor them to the ground. If lower branches are pruned off, the trees look top heavy. Most pines, whose lower branches often die naturally from being shaded, look appealing with bare lower trunks because their form is airier and more irregular.

Rarely should you remove healthy low branches—they do not grow back! Sometimes lower branches, shaded by those above or suffering from disease, die back on their own.

When this happens, prune them off at the trunk just outside the branch collar. Use good cultural practices—for example, irrigating, fertilizing, mulching, and pruning dead, broken, or dying branches—to keep lower branches alive and healthy.

PRUNING TECHNIQUES FOR NARROWLEAF EVERGREEN SHRUBS

The most commonly planted narrowleaf evergreen shrubs are yew, juniper, arborvitae, and false cypress. Popular as foundation plants, these shrubs often need yearly pruning to control their size. To save time and energy, plant dwarf and slow-growing varieties, which need less attention but are more expensive because of the time it takes for them to reach a saleable size in nurseries.

Proper pruning can dramatically control plant size for many years as demonstrated by two identical yews grown in Ohio. A yew planted in 1945 at the Ohio State Agricultural Research and Development Center and left unpruned grew to exceed 27 feet wide and 7 feet tall in 32 years. With yearly thinning, a similar plant reached only 5 feet wide and 2½ feet tall. The pruned shrub occupied its place in a home landscape for decades, but if it had been left unpruned it would have outgrown the space during its first 10 or 15 years.

Keep yews and other narrowleaf evergreens compact and natural-looking by thinning the long branches back to a side branch.

Repeat this thinning every year or two as needed to maintain the correct size.

The best time to prune is just before new growth begins in spring. In mid to late summer shorten long stems that arise from a second flush of growth. Do not prune heavily in summer; new growth may not sprout until spring and the exposed pruning cuts will look unsightly. It is best to prune these evergreens early enough in the growing season so that new growth can quickly fill in.

Thin; Don't Shear

The thinning cut is, once again, the best way to prune. Avoid using hedge shears unless pruning a formal hedge. With one hand lift up the branch that is to be pruned; with pruning shears in the other hand, reach beneath the branch into the shrub. Cut the branch at the point where it meets a side branch or the parent stem. The pruning cut should be camouflaged by longer, overhanging branches. With this method the foliage is not damaged, as happens when hedge shears are used for pruning.

Remove up to one quarter of the branches every year by thinning. Cut back to a parent stem or side branch that is at least two thirds the diameter of the branch being removed; such a branch is needed to assume apical control and maintain an orderly growth pattern. Thinning does not stimulate excessive growth as does shearing, so shrubs pruned by thinning require less attention from the gardener. Arborvitae and false cypress seldom produce

Left: Formal yew hedges need pruning with hedge shears several times a year to keep the flush of new growth from looking ragged. Right: To use hand shears properly on a needled evergreen, such as this juniper, reach into the interior of the shrub and cut the stem just beyond where the side branches emerge.

Shingle-Cutting a Spreading Shrub

To maintain the natural spreading shape of such plants as juniper, use thinning cuts to emphasize the shingled appearance of the branches. Make the upper branch layers the shortest and cut less from lower branches.

new buds on old bare wood. When thinning these plants always cut back to a small branch or green shoot.

Most narrowleaf evergreens can be thinned with hand pruners to create a natural-looking shingled effect. Thin the upper branch layers the shortest and cut progressively less from the lower layers. (Although shorter, the upper branches receive the most sunlight and grow faster than those at the bottom.) This method exposes the lower branches to the sun, encouraging them to remain thick with green needles. Shrubs of any shape—spreading, rounded, or conical—can be shingled. In addition to creating a neat, controlled, and natural appearance, thinning opens up the shrub to sunlight, keeping interior branches and shoots healthy, and makes it easier to spray for pests.

Pruning Upright Narrowleaf Evergreen Shrubs

Upright evergreen shrubs can be pruned yearly to maintain a controlled, dense, symmetrical, pyramidal shape. Thin outward-growing branches to an inward-growing side stem, which will grow upward and outward toward the light. Maintain one dominant leader; subordinate challenging leaders by thinning them to side branches. To reduce height, cut the dominant leader or multiple leaders to an inward-growing lateral. Shingle the side cuts as described above. Remove longer sections of branches at the top than at the base to maintain the tapering shape.

Pruning Foundation Plantings

Narrowleaf evergreens such as yew, juniper, arborvitae, and false cypress are traditionally used as foundation plants. Many broadleaf evergreens such as rhododendron, andromeda,

Shingle-Cutting an Upright Shrub

Taper an upright shrub from top to bottom with thinning cuts hidden beneath neighboring foliage; this maintains the layers of shingled branches that give the shrub a soft but uniform look.

azalea, and holly are also commonly planted. Evergreen shrubs provide year-round greenery, hide the foundation, and blend the house into the landscape. However, they often grow too large, obscuring windows and rubbing against the siding. Yearly pruning is necessary to keep most foundation shrubs in bounds.

Although evergreen foundation plants are often sheared, thinning is a better technique. Shearing encourages a shrub to grow slightly larger every year; a sheared shrub eventually gets too big for a foundation planting and develops a thin shell of foliage with a bare center. Shearing is more appropriate for topiary or a formal hedge. Thinning narrowleaf evergreen shrubs keeps them compact almost indefinitely and promotes dense growth and a more pleasing appearance.

Corrective Pruning of a New Hemlock

Before corrective pruning

After corrective pruning

Evergreens that have been sheared at the nursery often have competitive leaders and a dense shell of foliage. Correct this by using handheld pruning shears to cut back competing leaders and thin the shell of branches to allow light into the shrub's interior.

Correcting Newly Planted Shrubs

Some commercial plant growers shear the tops and sides of evergreens into a tight shape, intending to develop a dense saleable plant quickly. The new tip growth that results from shearing does not regenerate the whole plant, but is concentrated only on the surface.

This kind of shrub needs corrective thinning during the first or second year after planting. Reach into the plant and thin some of the closely spaced side branches. This allows more light into the center of the plant and encourages more natural growth and a less rigid outline. By the third year the shrub will have a looser shape.

PRUNING BROADLEAF EVERGREEN SHRUBS

The techniques for pruning most broadleaf evergreens are similar to those described for deciduous shrubs in the chapter "Pruning Deciduous Shrubs and Vines," page 43. Thin to reduce height and control size. Prune lightly just before flowering or more heavily right after, if the flowering effect is important.

Never use hedge shears to prune broadleaf evergreens that have large leaves. Cutting through the foliage disfigures it and results in an unsightly shrub. Broadleaf evergreens with fine-textured foliage—for example, boxwood or Japanese holly—can be sheared into a formal hedge without ill effect.

Rejuvenating a Rhododendron

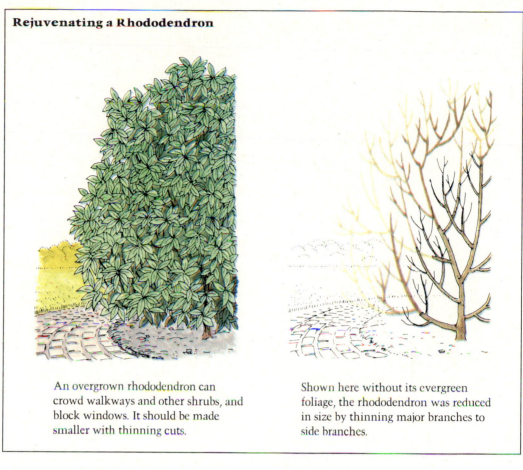

An overgrown rhododendron can crowd walkways and other shrubs, and block windows. It should be made smaller with thinning cuts.

Shown here without its evergreen foliage, the rhododendron was reduced in size by thinning major branches to side branches.

Rejuvenating Broadleaf Evergreen Shrubs

As with most other plants, broadleaf evergreens can grow too large for their landscape space. Regular thinning controls height and width. A leggy, overgrown shrub can usually be rejuvenated over several years by drastic pruning in late winter or early spring. Every year for three or four years cut back about one third of the oldest stems to the ground or thin tall stems back to lower side branches. This gradually reduces height and encourages new shoots to develop.

Occasionally an entire plant can be rejuvenated in one step by cutting all the branches back to just above the ground and letting new branches emerge. This technique only works on healthy vigorous plants.

Special Pruning for Rhododendrons and Relatives

Rhododendrons, azaleas, andromeda, and mountain laurel are closely related plants belonging to the family Ericaceae. These ericaceous plants, as they are called, are broadleaf evergreens noted for their beautiful flowers.

When planted very close together or too near a building, these popular landscape plants often outgrow their space allotment.

To produce compact plants with more flowers, pinch the tips of the new growth. To increase the number of trusses or flower clusters for the next year, pinch off about 1 inch of the new growth when it reaches 4 inches long and before leaves expand fully. Two or three new shoots will sprout from each shoot pinched. Pinch again right after the new shoots emerge, but before the next season's flower buds are formed.

Even with pinching, rhododendrons, andromeda, and mountain laurel eventually can become too tall and leggy; some azaleas reach huge sizes. Shorten long branches by thinning to a fork, a side branch, or a dormant or latent bud. Although difficult to see, growth buds appear all along the stems of ericaceous plants; cutting just above a bud causes a new shoot to emerge.

To renew an ericaceous plant, gradually thin it at the base over several years. The entire plant can also be cut off at ground level and allowed to resprout; it will take several

Opposite: To keep a neat but soft-edged appearance, prune small-leaved broadleaf evergreens, such as this Japanese holly, with hand shears.

Deadheading a Rhododendron

Remove faded flower trusses by bending them over and gently snapping them off between thumb and forefinger.

Pinching a Rhododendron

When new growth is about 4'' long and leaves still immature, pinch off about 1'' of the stem just above a set of leaves.

Pinching encourages branching and, therefore, profuse flowering because each branch tip usually produces a flower truss.

years for the plant to reach an attractive size and shape. This drastic, sometimes risky, measure works only for vigorous shrubs; very weak plants may not resprout.

Many ericaceous shrubs, such as mountain laurel, rhododrendrons, and andromeda, produce flowers grouped together into trusses. These plants grow more vigorously and flower better the following year if the old flowers are removed just after they fade and before they set seed. To remove the spent flower trusses, hold the branch with the faded flowers in one hand and with the other hand carefully snap off the flower head with a slight sideways pressure. Take care not to break off the buds or shoots along the sides of the trusses, because these will grow into branches tipped with the next year's flower buds.

Although most rhododendrons today are propagated by rooted cuttings, old specimens may be grafted. Grafted plants consist of two different plants joined together; a desirable cultivar forms the top growth and the roots are selected for their vigor. If suckers emerge below the graft union (visible as a swollen area at the base of the trunk), cut them cleanly away or snap them off where they attach to the understock. If left unchecked, suckers can overgrow the grafted cultivar and produce inferior flowers.

EVERGREEN HEDGES

As with deciduous shrubs, evergreens can be planted and pruned as either formal or informal hedges, depending upon the landscape design. Care must be taken while pruning to avoid damaging the foliage.

Formal Hedges

The main reason to shear conifers and fine-textured broadleaf evergreens is to shape and maintain them as formal hedges. Shear a hedge before growth begins in spring so that the flush of new growth covers the pruning cuts. The plant can also be sheared during or after the first growth spurt. Continue shaping evergreen hedges as needed, but stop early enough in the season for the new growth to mature and harden before freezing weather arrives. Keep the base wider and taper the sides to a narrower top. Follow the instructions for pruning deciduous formal hedges (see page 51), with the following exceptions.

Shearing a Yew

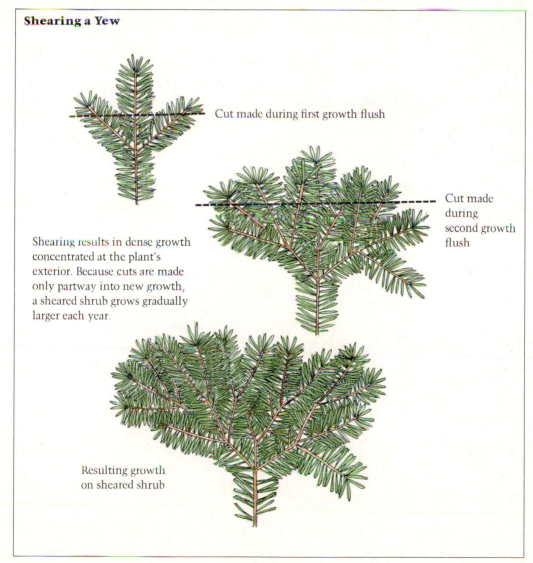

Cut made during first growth flush

Cut made during second growth flush

Shearing results in dense growth concentrated at the plant's exterior. Because cuts are made only partway into new growth, a sheared shrub grows gradually larger each year.

Resulting growth on sheared shrub

Left: Pruned with hand shears to retain its graceful branching structure, this informal hemlock hedge provides a barrier and a privacy screen for a side yard. Right: Sheared into a living wall of foliage, this boxwood visually extends the lines of the concrete walls, creating a pleasing geometrical effect.

Left: This informal hedge of Japanese holly has not been pruned for a year and is crowding the patio. Right: By cutting individual branches with hand shears, the hedge is greatly reduced in size but still retains its soft edges.

With conifers, at planting time cut back long leaders but otherwise do not prune them until two years after planting. Do not prune pine, spruce, or fir deeper than into the current season's growth; few, if any, buds develop on older wood and recovery is limited. Arborvitae and false cypress resprout from old wood that still has foliage. Prune pine hedges by cutting back new growth before it hardens. Use hand pruners to cut pines before the needles unfold; hedge shears will cause the needles to develop unattractive brown tips. Hedge shears can be used to prune spruce and fir hedges after the growth hardens in midsummer or before new growth begins in spring.

Yew and juniper, which have a longer growing season than other narrowleaf evergreens, often need pruning at least twice during the growing season to retain a neat, formal look. Prune these hedges just after the first flush of spring growth and then again after the second flush in midsummer. They can also be pruned in late summer but little regrowth will emerge to hide the cut stems. New growth arising from sheared shrubs such as yew and juniper is especially fast, thick, and vigorous. When sheared these shrubs increase in both height and spread each year; they may eventually outgrow their usefulness in the garden.

Using hedge shears on broadleaf evergreens—especially those with large leaves—disfigures and damages the foliage, provoking the wounded edges to brown. If shearing is an absolute necessity, then do it before plants actively begin to grow in spring; the flush of new growth will hide the damage.

Informal Hedges

For a soft, natural look, thin evergreens into an informal hedge using hand pruners. Not only does this avoid disfiguring the foliage, but it permits a more flexible pruning schedule. Except for pines, which must be pruned before the new growth hardens, evergreen hedges can be thinned anytime. Thinning allows sunlight deep within the hedge, keeping the inner foliage alive and green.

Rejuvenating a Hedge

It may or may not be possible to completely rejuvenate an overgrown hedge. Healthy boxwood, azaleas, rhododendrons, pyracantha, andromeda, and other broadleaf evergreens usually resprout at the base when all the stems are cut off in early spring or when one fourth to one third of the oldest stems are removed each year. If pruned in early spring before new growth begins, yew responds well to this kind of renewal treatment. Do not wait to cut back until summer, because the hedge may die. Many other narrowleaf evergreens resprout only from wood that bears visible buds or still has some foliage, so be cautious about pruning them drastically.

Pine, spruce, fir, and other needled evergreens do not resprout if cut back severely. The only way to renew them is to cut back to a whorl of branches on a main or side stem; new growth will emerge from existing buds and remaining branches. By repeating this procedure for several years, it is possible to gradually lower the height and narrow the width.

TOPIARY

Topiary is living sculpture—plants pruned into fanciful shapes such as animals or geometrical forms. Topiary can be a garden focal point and a conversation piece; however, it demands skillful pruning and constant care.

Although many trees and shrubs can be pruned into topiaries, fine-textured evergreens such as boxwood and yew are the most versatile. When using larger or coarser plants, stick to simple geometrical forms. Begin with a small, full, and dense plant. As with a hedge, shear frequently to confine and direct growth into a definite pattern.

Creating a topiary takes years of patient pruning and shearing. A double-ball shape, for example, will take 5 years if sculpted from holly or privet, and 10 years from yew. Expect to wait twice as long to create an animal or bird shape.

The double-ball or poodle is an easy topiary for a beginner. After shearing to form the lower ball, select several strong central branches and let them grow at least 2 feet above the first ball. Keep the straightest, most promising branch and remove the others. Strip the foliage from the bottom 12 inches of the emerging branch to form the stem that separates the two balls. Begin to shape the other 12 inches of growth into a second ball by heading it back to force side branches to form, and then shear the tips of these into a ball shape. Consult a specialized book on topiary for more details on this and other forms.

PRUNING EVERGREEN TREES

Evergreen trees such as spruce, fir, holly, pine, and southern magnolia can grow to great heights in the wild. They usually remain smaller in a garden, but may still grow too tall for the average home landscape unless pruned to restrict their size. These trees can be allowed to grow unhindered in a large open space; if planted close to a building or another tree, they must be pruned to control their growth.

Prune during the dormant season to restrict the size of an evergreen tree. Thin the

longest branches to side branches using hand pruners or loppers. If necessary, use an extension pole to reach overhead branches. The techniques for pruning broadleaf evergreen trees are similar to those described in "Pruning Deciduous Trees," page 21.

SPECIAL REQUIREMENTS OF NEEDLED EVERGREENS

Needled evergreens consist of pines, whose needles are arranged in bundles of 2, 3, or 5, and single-needled types, whose needles are not grouped but line the stems individually. These two kinds of needled evergreens have slightly different growth patterns and pruning needs.

Pines

Yearly pruning of pines can be limited to cutting back the candle growth partway. Heading a new candle forces the tree to develop terminal and lateral buds in a cluster at the ends of each cut; these buds grow the next year. Continual pinching or cutting back of the candles produces a densely branched tree. Be sure to prune before the stems of the new candles harden. Scotch pine hardens late and allows more leeway; white pine hardens early and the stems may die back if not pruned in time.

When pruning the terminal candles on pines, don't cut straight across; slant the cut at a 45-degree angle. This angling minimizes the possibility of double leaders forming just below the cut, because a new bud will form at the farthest tip of the cut.

Elegant and neatly pruned, these double-ball topiaries create a focal point that echoes the softer-edged, rounded shapes of the garden.

When only a portion of new growth is removed each year, large-growing trees will continue to increase in height and width. Eventually a pine can grow beyond its usefulness in the garden. To forestall this, thin long branches to side branches. This probably will eliminate new growth from a main branch, while allowing side branches to continue growing normally. Thin the main trunk this way to restrict the tree's size; a lateral branch will take over as the new leader. A less drastic measure calls for thinning into two-year-old wood early in the spring; new terminal buds will develop and grow the following season. Red, Austrian, and Scotch pines can be depended upon to produce new terminals when thinned in this manner.

Most conifers produce prominent branch collars. If a large living or dead limb must be removed, be sure to cut it off just to the outside of the collar; do not cut into the collar because the wound may not close over.

Single-Needled Evergreens

Spruce, fir, hemlock, Douglas fir, and other coniferous trees with short, single needles, grow large just as pines do. Keeping them small by pruning is a continual task of pinching or cutting back new growth each year. For natural-looking results use hand pruners, not hedge shears. As with pines, single-needled conifers seldom resprout from old wood.

New growth on these conifers emerges each year primarily from one-year-old buds of the previous season's growth. The growth produces a whorl of side branches just below the leader. Sometimes these conifers grow so rapidly that gaps develop between the whorls of branch layers. Prevent this disfiguring problem by shortening the leader each spring. Just beneath the cut, new terminal and lateral buds will develop into short stems and eventually into branches. Cut leaders approximately by half to a visible side bud or side shoot. Rub off any additional terminal buds to discourage multiple leaders from forming. If necessary cut back lower side branches to a bud or shoot to maintain a pyramidal taper.

Single-needled conifers permit a more flexible pruning schedule than do pines. Prune anytime from late summer, after growth has hardened, to just before new growth begins in spring.

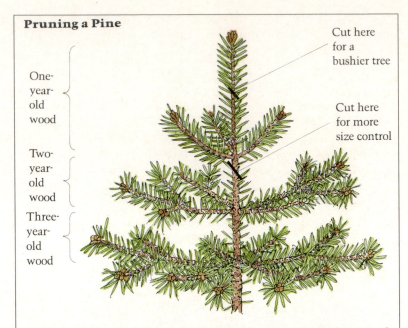

Pruning a Pine

One-year-old wood

Two-year-old wood

Three-year-old wood

Cut here for a bushier tree

Cut here for more size control

Pines produce a whorl of new growth each year, so age can be determined by counting the whorls of branches. Do not cut into wood older than two years, since it will not resprout. Pruning in spring into one- or two-year-old wood can control size without hurting the tree's appearance.

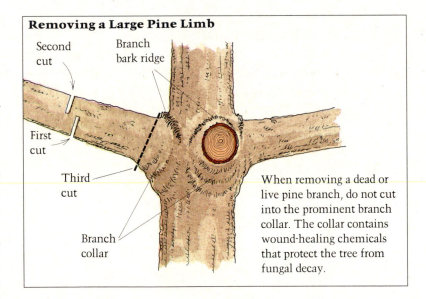

Removing a Large Pine Limb

Second cut

Branch bark ridge

First cut

Third cut

Branch collar

When removing a dead or live pine branch, do not cut into the prominent branch collar. The collar contains wound-healing chemicals that protect the tree from fungal decay.

Training Young Needled Evergreens

Conifers such as spruce, pine, fir, and hemlock should develop a single leader with layers of branches spreading like a pyramid below. If the leader is injured or broken, a new leader normally develops from a bud or lateral stem near the terminal. Sometimes several leaders form. It's best to remove or cut back the competing leaders promptly, although in most cases, one vertical stem will eventually dominate. If a leader does not form, bend a side branch at the top of the tree upward and support it with a wooden or metal stake.

A quickly growing pine, spruce, or fir may develop a leader that is disproportionately long, making the tree appear stretched. Before growth has hardened reduce the new leader to about 12 inches long for a denser, more compact tree. If a double leader forms remove one competing leader the following year. To maintain a graceful tapering shape, also cut back the upper lateral branches to 4 inches shorter than the leader. A pole pruner or ladder may be needed to reach the top of the tree.

An evergreen tree that has been sheared in the nursery—a balled-and-burlapped Christmas tree, for example—will naturally outgrow this imposed shape in a few years if it is not sheared again. If desired, thin some branches to let light into the interior, control size, and create a less rigid outline. Continued shearing causes the tree to grow gradually taller and wider since cuts are made only into the current or previous season's wood. Follow the procedure for rejuvenating evergreen shrubs (see page 30). After the first remedial thinning, the change in form will become apparent.

Rejuvenating Old Needled and Narrowleaf Evergeens

Most overgrown conifers are difficult to renew because dormant and latent buds are viable for only a few years. Adventitious buds seldom form. One way to reduce overall size of pine, spruce, arborvitae, yew, and juniper trees involves drop crotching as described on page 30.

Start pruning at the top of the tree and work downward and around. Prune side branches back to a side whorl and shorten upper branches more than lower branches to maintain the conical outline. Expect the tree to take three to five years to recover from this drastic pruning. New growth will emerge from the existing terminal buds on the lateral branches; a side branch will eventually become the new central leader. Unless the tree is healthy and vital to the landscape design, it may be better to replace the tree entirely.

Regular thinning and pruning while an evergreen is developing and maturing keeps it compact and dense. Avoid ever having to rejuvenate or remove an overgrown evergreen tree by properly controlling its growth from an early age.

Christmas Tree Pruning

To create a dense compact tree, each year Christmas tree growers cut the top leader of spruce and fir back to 10 to 14 inches and remove competing leaders. They make the terminal cut ⅜ to ½ inch above one good large side bud, which will develop into the new leader, and cut or rub off other nearby buds to prevent multiple leaders from forming. The growers shear or prune the remaining side branches to shape the tree during late summer or winter after new growth hardens and before the next season's growth begins. They are not concerned about pruning to a specific bud on these cuts.

On pines the cuts are made before new growth hardens, so that new buds form during that growing season. The growers prune the central leader back to 10 to 14 inches long when it expands fully but before the stem hardens. Then all the other lateral candles are cut 4 inches shorter than the central leader. Candles on lower branches are cut as needed to make a symmetrical, tapered pyramid.

These growers often use knives and hedge shears; in less experienced hands these tools may give the tree a severe appearance and can easily

damage the ends of the needles. It is better to use hand pruners. If the tree grows too tall to prune from the ground, use a pole pruner or stepladder.

Abies concolor (white fir)

Acacia melanoxylon (black acacia)

EVERGREEN TREE PRUNING ENCYCLOPEDIA

This encyclopedia provides pruning instructions for the most commonly grown evergreen trees. They are listed alphabetically by botanical name. If you don't know the botanical name of the tree, look up the common name in the index; there you will find the scientific name provided.

Abies species
Fir

These densely needled conifers growing 50 feet or taller are symmetrical with a strong central leader.

How to prune   Firs seldom need pruning except to remove dead or broken branches. If bottom branches spread too wide, thin to contain them. Don't cut back into leafless wood or the whole branch may die. Avoid topping, which will produce an unnatural, multiple-leader tree. If two leaders form when the tree is young, remove the weaker. For a specimen leave the lower branches to the ground.

When to prune   From late summer to just before growth begins in spring.

Acacia baileyana
Bailey acacia, golden mimosa

This relatively short-lived, single- or multiple-trunked broadleaf evergreen tree reaches 30 feet tall and about as wide.

How to prune   When the tree is young, remove narrow, V-shaped crotches that become weaker with age. For multiple trunks, thin top growth to lateral branches to encourage lower branches. For a single-trunked tree remove suckers. Mature specimens often become very dense. Thin to open the center of the crown and remove deadwood.

When to prune   Can prune anytime, but pruning after the flush of spring growth provides maximum control.

Acacia melanoxylon
Black acacia, blackwood acacia

Fast-growing, this relatively short-lived broadleaf evergreen commonly reaches 35 feet tall and as wide.

How to prune   When young eliminate narrow crotches before they cause problems. It may be necessary to head young trees to promote a wide spread. Thin mature trees and eliminate deadwood.

When to prune   Late dormant season or after blooming.

Arbutus menziesii
Madrone

A roundheaded broadleaf evergreen tree or large shrub, madrone can reach 80 feet tall but more commonly grows around 30 feet. It is a very strong tree when established.

How to prune   Remove deadwood and interior branches to expose the attractive bark.

When to prune   Late dormant season.

Calocedrus decurrens
California incense cedar, incense cedar

A symmetrical narrowleaf conifer growing 50 to 70 feet tall and 15 to 30 feet wide at the base, incense cedar produces scalelike foliage in flat sprays.

How to prune   The tree is most beautiful if left to assume its natural form. Do not remove low branches or top. Can be sheared into a hedge.

When to prune   Dormant season.

Casuarina equisetifolia
Horsetail tree, beefwood

Horsetail tree is not a conifer although it is often mistaken for a pine. What appear to be needles are actually green scaly stems. It grows 50 feet tall and 20 feet wide.

How to prune   Seldom needs pruning. If a young tree develops several trunks, select the best and remove the others. Cut out dead or broken branches annually. Tolerates shearing into a formal hedge.

When to prune   Anytime.

Cedrus deodara (deodar cedar)

Chamaecyparis lawsoniana 'Aurea Minima' (Lawson cypress)

Cedrus atlantica
Atlas cedar

Forming a broad-spreading crown when mature, this needled conifer grows 40 to 60 feet tall and 30 to 40 feet wide.

How to prune Maintain a central leader as long as practical; competing leaders tend to split off, particularly if ice- or snow-laden. Remove deadwood and weak branches lying against stronger ones. Lowest branches can be removed to expose the silvery bark.

When to prune Late dormant season.

Cedrus deodara
Deodar cedar

This needled conifer has a pyramidal shape, semipendulous branches, and a nodding top. It grows 40 to 70 tall and slightly narrower at the base.

How to prune Maintain compactness by cutting new growth back by half in the late spring. Remove deadwood. The tree tolerates shearing. It will not resprout from old leafless wood.

When to prune Late dormant season for major pruning; after spring flush of growth to maintain density and compactness.

Cephalotaxus fortunei
Chinese plum yew

A small tree or shrub growing 10 to 30 feet tall, this narrowleaf conifer resembles a true yew. It usually produces two or three upright limbs bearing horizontal branches that give the tree a layered appearance.

How to prune Thin to maintain the desired shape. New growth will emerge from even the oldest wood.

When to prune Late dormant season.

Chamaecyparis species
False cypress

A narrowleaf conifer with scalelike foliage, false cypress grows in a narrow pyramid that can reach 100 feet tall. Many cultivars are available for use as trees or shrubs. Lawson cypress, *C. lawson-*

iana, can be sheared into a formal hedge.

How to prune Little pruning is needed. Clean out deadwood and debris that collect on the interior branches. Control height and width with thinning cuts. False cypress will not resprout from bare wood; buds, however, are located on older wood that has foliage.

When to prune Late dormant season; anytime for touch-up pruning.

Cinnamomum camphora
Camphor tree

This broadleaf evergreen grows slowly to 50 feet tall with a wide-spreading crown.

How to prune When young, direct scaffold branches outward rather than upward for the most attractive mature form. When older, remove dead or damaged wood and suckers.

When to prune Late dormant season for major pruning; anytime for smaller cuts.

Cupressus arizonica
Arizona cypress

This narrowleaf conifer is pyramidal when young but eventually develops a broad, open crown; grows 40 to 70 feet tall.

How to prune Avoid heavy pruning since cypress wood is slow to recover from pruning. Encourage a single leader and remove dead, broken, or diseased branches.

When to prune Late dormant season to early summer.

Cupressus macrocarpa
Monterey cypress

Conical when young, this narrowleaf conifer becomes spreading and more open when older. It grows 40 to 50 feet tall and 20 to 30 feet wide.

How to prune It's best to leave the tree in its natural form, although it can be sheared into a formal hedge. Yellowing leaves that turn dark red indicate a fungus; remove diseased branches.

When to prune Spring and early summer, if at all. Winter pruning can be fatal.

Eucalyptus ficifolia (scarlet-flowering gum)

Laurus nobilis (sweet bay)

Cupressus sempervirens
Italian cypress

Narrow, strongly fastigiate varieties of this narrowleaf conifer are most common.

How to prune It needs little pruning except to remove dead twigs girdled by twig borers.

When to prune Late dormant season to early summer.

Eucalyptus ficifolia
Scarlet-flowering gum, flaming gum

This small eucalyptus, forming a round head about 25 feet tall and wide, blooms profusely in summer.

How to prune Because the tree tends to be low-branching, thin bottom limbs to promote a higher crown and a taller single trunk. The tree can also be trained as a multitrunked specimen. Remove suckers and dead or broken branches. Prune off large seed pods after flowering.

When to prune Early spring.

Ilex aquifolium
Holly, English holly, Christmas holly

This broadleaf evergreen, which grows 40 feet or taller, has prickly leaves.

How to prune Holly is adaptable to many different pruning treatments including shearing. To train as a tree, select a single leader when young and then thin vigorous branches as necessary.

When to prune Late dormant season; Christmastime if using clippings for indoor decorations.

Ilex opaca
American holly

A broadleaf tree, American holly forms a pyramid that can reach 50 feet tall. The leaves are spiny.

How to prune Prune when transplanting to promote the dominance of a single leader and thin for pyramidal habit. Later, thin individual branches as needed to maintain shape. For a specimen tree allow the lower branches to remain. Remove them to feature the bark or trunk. American holly can withstand heavy pruning and shearing.

When to prune Late dormant season is best; it can also be pruned at other times (heavy pruning after flowering or during summer may reduce berries).

Laurus nobilis
Grecian laurel, bay, bay laurel, laurel, sweet laurel, sweet bay

This multitrunked broadleaf evergreen, the source of bay leaves used in cooking, grows slowly into a compact, almost conical form about 25 feet tall. Easily shaped, Grecian laurel can adapt to even the severe pruning of topiary. It can also be sheared to create a formal hedge or thinned for an informal hedge.

How to prune Control speed and shape of growth by shearing or thinning heavily before new growth begins. If removing the lower branches to expose the trunk, expect prolific suckering.

When to prune Late dormant season.

Magnolia grandiflora
Southern magnolia, bull bay

This broadleaf evergreen can reach 80 feet tall with branches to the ground.

How to prune Not much pruning is needed once the tree is established. When young develop the main framework. Remove interior water sprouts as they form. For better flowering thin lightly in early spring.

When to prune Late dormant season is best; it can also be pruned at other times.

Maytenus boaria
Mayten

This graceful broadleaf evergreen with semipendulous branches grows slowly to about 40 feet tall with a 20-foot spread.

How to prune Train to either single or multiple trunks as desired. Remove suckers, periodically thin the crown, and trim low hanging branches if necessary.

When to prune Late dormant season.

Picea pungens 'Glauca' (Colorado blue spruce)

Pinus strobus (white pine)

Olea europaea
Olive tree

Since this broadleaf evergreen tolerates heavy pruning, it can be used as a tree, shrub, or hedge. It eventually reaches 20 to 30 feet tall. For ornamental use only, select fruitless varieties such as 'Swan Hill'.

How to prune   To train as a tree, thin side branches below the point where the main scaffold branches to begin. For multiple trunks, select five or fewer strong suckers and train them in a desirable direction. Excessive pruning encourages prolific, unattractive growth; avoid this by thinning lightly each year.

When to prune   Anytime; wait until after fruiting for maximum olive crop.

Picea species
Spruce

These needled conifers are pyramidal, growing 50 to 100 feet tall and about a third as wide.

How to prune   Other than having an occasional dead branch removed, these trees require little pruning. To stimulate denser habit, cut new growth back about halfway. If the leader is lost at a young age, select and train a new one. Although the lowest branches can be removed for clearance, the tree will look best with branches to the ground.

When to prune   Late summer to late dormant season.

Pinus bungeana
Lacebark pine

A slow-growing needled conifer that can reach 75 feet tall, laceback pine often has multiple trunks.

How to prune   Remove lower limbs to show off the beautiful flaking bark on the trunk. As with all pines, old leafless wood will not resprout; cut back limb only to a fork in the branch. Cut back candle growth partway each year to develop compact, dense habit.

When to prune   Afer candles elongate but before needles expand in spring.

Pinus halepensis
Aleppo pine

Relatively slow to start but then growing quickly to 50 feet, this needled conifer has an open branching pattern with a rounded top and short branches. It may become sparse and spindly with age.

How to prune   As with other pines, pinch candles before the needles enlarge to stimulate more compact and dense growth. Never leave a branch stub without needles or side branches. Remove deadwood.

When to prune   After the candles elongate but before needles expand in spring; anytime to remove deadwood.

Pinus nigra
Black pine, Austrian pine

See *Pinus sylvestris*

Pinus radiata
Monterey pine

Very fast-growing to between 60 and 100 feet tall, this needled conifer is pyramidal when young but becomes rounded with age.

How to prune   Monterey pine tolerates enough pruning to be useful as a hedge. To control size pinch back candles before the needles show. To slow growth, cut candles back by two thirds. Pines have few latent buds so never leave a branch stub.

When to prune   After the candles elongate but before needles expand in spring.

Pinus strobus
Eastern white pine, white pine

See *Pinus sylvestris*

Pinus sylvestris
Scotch pine

These rapidly growing needled conifers become 50 to 70 feet tall; cultivars with dwarf and weeping forms are also available. Tree forms are pyramidal when young, becoming open and irregular with age.

How to prune   Although these pines seldom require pruning, their growth can be slowed when young by shearing to a pyramidal shape. They can also be sheared into hedges and windbreaks. Guidelines for other pines apply to these species.

When to prune   After the candles elongate but before needles expand in spring.

Pseudotsuga menziesii (Douglas fir)

Quercus virginiana (live oak)

Pyrus kawakamii (evergreen pear)

Prunus caroliniana
Cherry laurel, Carolina laurel cherry, mock orange

A broadleaf evergreen that can be grown as a tree or a shrub, cherry laurel reaches 18 to 40 feet tall.

How to prune To train cherry laurel as a small tree, when young, select wide-angled scaffolds and prune to shape. It can also be sheared into a formal hedge or topiary.

When to prune For a formal shape, prune after new growth in spring and again in the fall. If the tree is allowed to grow naturally, prune in the late dormant season.

Prunus lusitanica
Portugal laurel

This broadleaf evergreen, growing to 30 feet tall, usually has multiple trunks.

How to prune Left natural, it needs little pruning. Formal shapes are easily maintained with frequent shearing.

When to prune Anytime.

Pseudotsuga menziesii
Douglas fir, Oregon pine

This needled conifer retains a graceful pyramidal shape for many years, eventually reaching 40 to 80 feet tall in a garden. It grows to 250 feet in the wild.

How to prune Maintain a central leader; if the natural leader is lost, train a new leader. Pinch new growth on horizontal limbs for more compact growth and less weight on the branches. If an older tree is topped, it will decline immediately. Young trees can be sheared into a formal hedge.

When to prune Late dormant season; after spring growth to slow the tree.

Pyrus kawakamii
Evergreen pear

Reaching 30 feet tall, this broadleaf evergreen is partly deciduous in very cold winter areas. It can be grown as a shrub or a small tree with an open irregular crown.

How to prune The natural multiple-trunked form is quite beautiful especially if laterals are thinned to expose the trunks. To train into a tree, select one trunk and choose laterals at the appropriate heights. Pinch back laterals to buds facing upward and outward to strengthen them. Evergreen pear can also be espaliered. Remove wood infected with fire blight, being sure to cut into healthy wood about 12 inches away.

When to prune After flowering.

Quercus agrifolia
California live oak, coast live oak

This picturesque wide-spreading broadleaf evergreen oak can reach 70 feet tall and 100 feet wide.

How to prune Until well established, prevent multiple leaders and branches from forming too close to the ground. Select wide-angled scaffolds (most are that way naturally) 10 to 12 feet above the ground. On mature specimens the most pruning required is to remove deadwood, crossing branches, or out-of-place limbs. Do not prune unnecessarily.

When to prune Early dormant season (do not prune in summer since that encourages powdery mildew infection).

Quercus virginiana
Live oak, southern live oak

This sturdily branched, wide-spreading broadleaf tree, growing to 60 feet tall, is usually evergreen but becomes partly deciduous at the northern limit of its range.

How to prune This massive oak has particularly strong limbs and often branches very close to the ground. Let it grow naturally and only prune correctively.

When to prune Late dormant season.

Schinus molle
California pepper tree, Peruvian pepper tree

A fine-textured broadleaf evergreen with weeping branches and a pleasing silhouette, this tree grows 30 to 40 feet tall.

Taxus cuspidata (yew)

Sequoia sempervirens (coast redwood)

Thuja plicata (western red cedar)

How to prune Since it grows into a large shrub if ignored, prune to maintain a single stem. Resist making cuts larger than 4 inches across if possible; cuts will bleed at any time of the year and are highly susceptible to wood-decay fungus diseases. Thin the crown frequently and lightly. This plant can be sheared into a 4-foot-high formal hedge.

When to prune Late dormant season for major cuts; anytime for touch-up pruning.

Sequoia sempervirens
Coast redwood, redwood

Dramatic and fast-growing, this pyramidal narrowleaf conifer reaches 60 feet tall in most gardens. It grows to 300 feet in nature.

How to prune Only corrective pruning is needed. Remove suckers. Redwood can be used as a hedge if planted close together and annually topped and trimmed.

When to prune Anytime.

Taxus species
Yew

These dense narrowleaf conifers are among the most widely used topiary and hedge plants. Species and cultivars are available ranging from conical trees to low-spreading shrubs. Choose a cultivar whose natural shape is suited to its planting location and less pruning will be needed.

How to prune Yews grow in two spurts of growth during spring and summer. They must be sheared at least twice a year for a formal appearance. Shearing, however, results in a thin shell of foliage on the plant's exterior and bare branches inside. For an informal hedge or specimen, thin once a year before new growth begins in the spring. Thin about a quarter of the old growth back to lateral branches.

For a natural tree shape, encourage the development of the central leader and prune laterals with thinning cuts. To rejuvenate, cut to within 6 to 12 inches of the ground in early spring before growth begins.

When to prune Dormant season for major pruning; anytime to shape and trim.

Thuja occidentalis
American arborvitae, northern white cedar, white cedar

This narrowleaf evergreen grows fairly slowly into a narrow pyramid about 45 feet tall. Several cultivars with globe or weeping forms are smaller.

How to prune If grown naturally, arborvitae only needs touch-up thinning. It is often used as a hedge; keep in mind that it does not resprout from bare wood. See pruning details given under *T. plicata*.

When to prune Late dormant season for major cuts; after spring growth for touch-up pruning.

Thuja plicata
Canoe cedar, giant arborvitae, giant cedar, western red cedar

Growing to 70 feet or more tall, this narrowleaf conifer bears its branches all the way to the ground.

How to prune Thin branches as needed if growing

as a tree. For a hedge or screen, let the plants grow a foot taller than the desired hedge height. Then top the leaders back to 6 inches below the desired height and thin laterals. This method creates a good top surface.

When to prune Late dormant season to shape; after spring growth until early summer for touch-up pruning.

Tsuga species
Hemlock

Among the most graceful needled evergreens, hemlocks develop into outstanding specimens up to 70 feet tall with slightly pendulous branches.

How to prune If grown as trees hemlocks need very little pruning. If the leader is lost, replace it by training a nearby branch upward. Hemlocks tolerate heavy shearing and can be maintained as a formal hedge or windbreak. They may also be thinned heavily for an informal hedge. Occasional thinning will also keep sheared hedges thicker.

When to prune Late dormant season.

Aucuba japonica (Japanese aucuba)

Abelia × *grandiflora* (glossy abelia)

Buxus sempervirens (common boxwood)

EVERGREEN SHRUB PRUNING ENCYCLOPEDIA

Described here are general pruning instructions for many of the most commonly grown coniferous and broadleaf evergreen shrubs. They are listed alphabetically according to botanical name. If you do not know the botanical name of the shrub, look up the common name in the index, where you will find the proper scientific name listed.

Abelia × grandiflora
Glossy abelia

Evergreen in mild-winter areas and deciduous in colder climates, this broadleaf shrub grows into a rounded form 10 feet tall and 8 feet wide. Glossy abelia flowers from midsummer until frost.

How to prune   Abelia flowers on the previous season's wood, but in areas with long growing seasons it also flowers most prolifically on new spring growth. Remove one third of the oldest growth annually to encourage new growth. Thin winter-killed branches. Abelia can be sheared but will lose most of the flowers and natural beauty. Rejuvenate by cutting almost to the ground.

When to prune   Dormant season.

Arbutus unedo
Strawberry tree, cane apple

This broadleaf shrub grows slowly to approximately 12 feet tall but may become as tall as 20 feet. It can be trained as a small tree.

How to prune   Usually grows into an interesting shape without pruning. Remove the lowest branches to reveal the bark, which becomes gnarled with age. If the crown becomes too dense, thin it.

When to prune   Late dormant season.

Arctostaphylos manzanita
Common manzanita, Parry manzanita

Varying in size from 6 to 20 feet tall with a spread of 10 or more feet, this broadleaf shrub can be treelike.

How to prune   It requires little or no pruning. If desired, prune to reveal the reddish bark or thin vigorous growth to prevent legginess.

When to prune   Late dormant season.

Aucuba japonica
Gold-dust plant, Japanese laurel, Japanese aucuba

The size of this broadleaf shrub, which grows moderately fast to 5 to 10 feet tall, can easily be controlled.

How to prune   If upright shoots become too floppy, head just above a new bud.

When to prune   Late dormant season for major cuts; after spring growth to shape lightly.

Azara microphylla
Boxleaf azara

This tender broadleaf evergreen grows 10 to 18 feet tall.

How to prune   Remove shoots with spent flowers in the late spring. This shrub can be informally trained or espaliered against a wall. Thin to outside laterals to control height. Replace an old trunk occasionally with a sucker.

When to prune   Late dormant season for major cuts; anytime for touch-up pruning.

Berberis julianae
Wintergreen barberry

See *Berberis verruculosa*

Berberis verruculosa
Warty barberry

These evergreen barberries are spiny broadleaf shrubs. *B. verruculosa* remains a compact 3-foot-tall mound and *B. julianae* grows to 7 feet.

How to prune   Thin older canes at the base every year.

When to prune   Late dormant season.

Buxus species
Box, boxwood

Broadleaf evergreens with dainty leaves, boxwoods can be sheared or left natural. They are popular hedges in formal gardens. Many cultivars; mature heights range from 1 foot to 6 feet.

Callistemon citrinus (lemon bottlebrush)

Daphne odora (winter daphne)

Erica species and *Calluna* species (heath and heather)

How to prune For a formal hedge shear the leading growth of young plants to produce the maximum number of branches. Boxwood can also be thinned for a handsome but more casual-looking hedge.

When to prune Late dormant season for all major pruning; anytime to maintain neatness and shape.

Callistemon citrinus
Lemon bottlebrush, crimson bottlebrush

This common, easily grown broadleaf shrub is often pruned to a single-stemmed tree about 12 feet tall.

How to prune It can be trained into a small tree, multitrunked shrub, or espalier. For best flowering cut back a little each year. Cut only into the leafy parts of the stem since bottlebrush doesn't resprout from bare wood. Leaving a bare stub may cause the branch to die.

When to prune Late dormant season or immediately after flowering.

Calluna species
Scotch heather, heather

See *Calluna and Erica*

Calluna and Erica
Heath, spring heath, heather

These fine-textured, low-spreading, flowering shrubs form twiggy mounds of needle-like foliage. They are often sheared into formal hedges. *Calluna* blooms in the late summer or fall; *Erica* blooms in late winter.

How to prune Cut back in early spring to stimulate dense new growth. They can be clipped back severely in early spring.

When to prune After flowers fade.

Camellia species
Camellia

These winter-flowering broadleaf evergreens can grow to 15 feet tall and wide.

How to prune Start shaping the plant when young to encourage dominance of a single stem with many branches.

Frequent pinching afterward keeps pruning problems to a minimum. Maintain shape by taking two or three leaves when cutting flowers. For the largest flowers remove all but one bud per cluster. Eliminate the others by piercing them from the tip of the bud downward; as air enters, the buds dry up and fall off.

To reduce size drastically, cut back branches in the late dormant season to one quarter their length. This forces buds to break along the stem. The following spring thin the top to the desired height.

When to prune Late dormant season for major cuts; anytime to shape.

Correa pulchella
Australian fuchsia, pink Australian fuschia

This tender broadleaf evergreen grows to 2 feet tall and 8 feet wide.

How to prune All this shrub requires is heading back the most vigorous growth to induce branching and greater denseness.

When to prune Anytime.

Cotoneaster species
Cotoneaster

See the *Cotoneaster* description in the deciduous shrub listing.

Cytisus species
Broom

See the *Cytisus* description in the deciduous shrub listing.

Daphne odora
Winter daphne

Growing to 4 feet tall and spreading even wider, this broadleaf evergreen produces fragrant spring flowers.

How to prune Cutting flowers to take indoors usually eliminates the need for any other pruning. Make cuts close to buds that face the direction growth should take. For a spreading shrub select buds facing upward and out. For vertical growth cut back to inward-facing buds.

When to prune After flowering.

Euonymus japonica (evergreen euonymus)

Ilex crenata (Japanese holly)

Dodonaea viscosa 'Purpurea'
Hopbush, purple hopseed

This purple-leaved shrub grows rapidly to 10 to 15 feet tall if left unpruned.

How to prune Where the shrub has sufficient room, no pruning is needed. Thin it to fit a restricted area. It tolerates shearing into a formal hedge. To train as a small, single-trunked tree select the most promising stem when young and head the shoots that emerge along it. As the trunk gains strength, remove the lower sprouts entirely.

When to prune Late dormant season.

Erica species
Heather

See *Calluna* and *Erica*

Escallonia species
Escallonia

These vigorous broadleaf evergreens have a dense, rounded, upright growth habit. Ranging in size from 3 to 15 feet tall, some of these flowering shrubs can be trained as small trees.

How to prune Escallonia gets leggy if pruning is neglected. It responds well to shearing into a formal hedge; thin for a more attractive shrub. Always prune back to a branch or visible bud.

When to prune Late dormant season.

Euonymus fortunei
Wintercreeper

Numerous cultivars of this broadleaf evergreen species are available; they range from vines to small shrubs.

How to prune This hardy plant can be trained as a spreading or climbing vine or shrub. Prune considerably every year. Shear it to an attractive ground cover or hedge. Remove deadwood and check for euonymus scale, a common pest. Sometimes wintercreeper can be rejuvenated by cutting back to the ground.

When to prune Late dormant season.

Euonymus japonica
Evergreen euonymus

This broadleaf shrub, growing to around 10 feet tall, is more upright than *E. fortunei*.

How to prune This euonymus can be trained into a small tree. Keep it thinned to maximize air circulation, which discourages mildew. Prune the branch tips to maintain compactness.

When to prune Late dormant season for major cuts; after spring growth to midsummer for light pruning.

Fatshedera lizei
Botanical-wonder, ivy tree

This vining broadleaf shrub can be trained to grow upright to a height of about 10 to 15 feet with a slightly greater spread.

How to prune For a bushier shrub prune the growing tips frequently. Fatshedera also makes a satisfactory ground cover, espalier, or vine. To rejuvenate cut to the ground.

When to prune Late dormant season for major cuts; anytime for touch-up pruning.

Gardenia jasminoides
Gardenia

This broadleaf shrub, growing to 6 feet tall, produces heavily scented flowers on new growth from spring though summer.

How to prune Requires little or no pruning. Thin to reshape as needed. Rejuvenate by cutting oldest stems to 8 inches above the ground in early spring.

When to prune Anytime.

Genista species
Broom

See the *Genista* description in the deciduous shrub listing.

Hebe species
Shrub veronica

These tender broadleaf shrubs make fairly fast-growing hedge plants. Most veronicas grow around 4 feet tall.

How to prune Remove faded flowers and seed capsules to reduce the drain on the plant's energy. Head to keep the shrub compact. To renew a neglected hedge remove one half of the old wood at the ground.

Juniperus scopulorum (Rocky Mountain juniper)

Kalmia latifolia (mountain laurel)

When to prune Late dormant season; if these shrubs are of borderline hardiness in an area, don't touch-up prune later than midsummer.

Ilex cornuta
Chinese holly

See *Ilex glabra*

Ilex crenata
Japanese holly, box-leaved holly

See *Ilex glabra*

Ilex glabra
Inkberry

Cultivars of these broadleaf evergreen holly species vary from one-foot-tall ground covers to large rounded shrubs. They make good foundation plants, shrub borders, or hedges.

How to prune Hollies generally grow into one of three habits: rounded and dense shrubs, open-growing border shrubs, or pyramidal trees. (Read about tree hollies in the evergreen tree listing.) Dense growers such as *I. cornuta*

and *I. crenata* can be sheared into formal hedges but they are much more attractive thinned as informal hedges. Do not shear *I. glabra*; thin as needed to shape.

When to prune Late dormant season; Christmastime if using clippings as indoor decoration (do not prune in subzero temperatures).

Juniperus species and cultivars
Juniper

These tough narrowleaf evergreens are among the most widely used shrubs. Species and cultivars range from inches high to 50 feet tall. To minimize pruning, choose the proper size and shape for the available space.

How to prune To limit young junipers, thin new growth almost to its point of origin. Make the cut just above a side shoot that's heading in the desired direction. Thin the top branches to prevent them from shading and killing lower branches and to maintain a layered appearance. Keep the shrub's natural shape in mind

and prune to maintain the feathery appearance. Rejuvenate by cutting out entire branches and cutting others back to where they branch. Drop crotch to reduce size of large vase-shaped shrubs.

When to prune Late dormant season.

Kalmia latifolia
Mountain laurel

This broadleaf ericaceous shrub or small tree flowers in early summer. It can grow 10 to 25 feet tall, sometimes becoming leggy.

How to prune Thin old and dead branches to induce new branching at the base. Pinch off fading flowers.

When to prune After flowering.

Laurus nobilis
Grecian laurel, bay, bay laurel, laurel, sweet laurel

See the *Laurus nobilis* description in the evergreen tree listing.

Ligustrum japonicum
Japanese privet, wax-leaf privet, privet

This reliable broadleaf evergreen makes an excellent screen or hedge. Unchecked it grows to 12 feet or more, but it can be kept much lower.

How to prune When training privet into a formal hedge, shear often throughout the summer to build a strong, wide base. Remove the oldest wood at the ground periodically. If grown as an informal shrub, it seldom requires pruning.

When to prune Late dormant season for major cutting; anytime to maintain shape.

Mahonia aquifolium
Oregon grape, mountain grape, holly mahonia, blue barberry, holly barberry

This hardy broadleaf evergreen has prickly leaves that somewhat resemble holly. It can grow up to 6 feet tall, but lower-growing cultivars are available.

Nandina domestica (heavenly bamboo)

Photinia serrulata (photinia)

How to prune As the plant matures, it develops several stems that are bare of leaves except at the top. Cut these stems back to the ground. Pinch new growth after flowering to encourage bushiness.

When to prune Late dormant season to remove stems; growing season to pinch or prune lightly.

Myoporum laetum 'Carsonii'
Myoporum

This fast-growing broadleaf evergreen, reaching about 15 feet tall, can be a small tree or a shrub. This cultivar normally keeps its leaves all the way to the ground.

How to prune If allowed to grow naturally, it needs little attention. If trained as a single or multitrunked tree, prune off lower branches to reveal the trunk and thin the crown annually to reduce wind resistance and top-heaviness. Cut back severely to rejuvenate.

When to prune Late dormant season is best; it can also be pruned at other times.

Myrtus communis
Myrtle, true myrtle

This fragrant-flowered broadleaf evergreen grows 5 to 10 feet tall.

How to prune Let this malleable plant form an irregular mound or prune it as desired. It can be thinned for an informal hedge or sheared into topiary or a formal hedge. To reduce height thin the tallest stems from inside the plant.

When to prune Anytime.

Nandina domestica
Heavenly bamboo, sacred bamboo

Usually evergreen, this broadleaf shrub loses its leaves—and can die to the ground—as temperatures approach zero. Upright and airy, it grows slowly to about 6 feet tall and 3 feet wide.

How to prune This plant looks best with annual thinning. Remove three or four of the oldest canes to the ground. To maintain at a constant height, continually pinch new top growth.

When to prune Late dormant season.

Osmanthus fragrans
Fragrant olive, tea olive, sweet olive

This fairly tender broadleaf plant can be trained as a tall shrub, small tree, hedge, or espalier.

How to prune It tolerates shearing into a formal hedge. Thin new growth frequently to develop an informal hedge or a specimen shrub.

When to prune Anytime.

Photinia species
Photinia

These broadleaf shrubs with attractive deep-red new foliage grow to around 10 feet tall and wide. Their primary use is as a hedge.

How to prune When young, train to multiple stems and thin the most vigorously growing ones. Clip two or more times per season to maintain shape and keep the new red-tinged leaves coming.

When to prune Growing season. (Avoid pruning in late summer near the northern border of this plant's hardiness.)

Pieris japonica
Andromeda, lily-of-the-valley bush

This leathery broadleaf evergreen can reach 8 to 9 feet tall and about half as wide. It bears white bell-shaped flowers on old wood.

How to prune Andromeda is easy to manage and seldom needs pruning. Remove faded flowers to encourage better blooming. Thin old growth on a specimen that has become too leggy.

When to prune After flowering.

Pittosporum tobira
Tobira, mock orange, Japanese pittosporum

Although it can grow to tree size, this shrub responds well to pruning and can be kept at almost any size.

How to prune Shear into a formal hedge or thin for an informal hedge or open multistemmed shrub.

When to prune Anytime.

Prunus laurocerasus (cherry laurel)

Xylosma congestum (shiny xylosma)

Rhododendron hybrid (rhododendron)

Prunus laurocerasus
English laurel, cherry laurel

This broadleaf evergreen grows 30 feet or taller where the climate is warm and the growing season is long. Elsewhere English laurel grows much shorter.

How to prune   In warm climates cut back frequently. Thin and prune to the shape desired for a specimen shrub or tree. English laurel can be thinned for a large-scale informal hedge. Cultivars with drooping branches respond well to espaliering.

When to prune   Anytime.

Raphiolepis indica
Indian hawthorn

This undemanding, leathery broadleaf evergreen is commonly used as an informal hedge. Its height varies depending upon the cultivar.

How to prune   Indian hawthorn needs little pruning. Pinch to encourage thick growth.

When to prune   Growing season.

Rhododendron species and cultivars
Rhododrendron, azalea

Members of the same large genus, rhododendrons and azaleas are broadleaf shrubs that vary considerably in height; they can be evergreen or deciduous, depending upon the species or cultivar.

How to prune   Remove faded flowers if flowers are borne in trusses. Thin to shape and control size. Maintain layered branching habit of horizontally branching azaleas. Do not shear azaleas as this removes flower buds and results in an unnatural-looking plant. Rejuvenate by cutting back one fifth to one third of stems to the ground over a period of three to five years. (See pages 69 and 70 for more details about pruning these plants.)

When to prune   After flowering or late dormant season.

Spartium species
Broom

See the *Cytisus* description in the deciduous shrub listing.

Taxus species
Yew

See the *Taxus* description in the evergreen tree listing.

Umbellularia californica
California bay, California laurel, myrtle, Oregon myrtle, pepperwood

In the wild this broadleaf evergreen grows 70 feet tall with an equal spread. It is usually smaller in cultivation.

How to prune   In the garden train to a single leader when young. Mature trees rarely need pruning other than to remove dead or diseased wood. Thin to reduce shade if desired.

When to prune   Late dormant season.

Vitex lucens
Chaste tree, New Zealand chaste tree

This broadleaf evergreen with a round, spreading form is a slow to moderate grower, eventually reaching 50 feet tall. It blooms on new growth.

How to prune   Train when young to a central leader with well-spaced scaffolds beginning around 10 feet high. When mature prune if necessary to remove damaged or out-of-place limbs.

When to prune   Dormant season.

Xylosma congestum
Shiny xylosma

This versatile broadleaf evergreen shrub is deciduous in cold-winter climates. It naturally forms an open, round, spreading plant about 10 feet tall and wide.

How to prune   Pruning is usually not required. It can be sheared into a formal hedge or topiary, thinned for an informal hedge, espaliered, or trained as a single- or multiple-stemmed tree. Lower branches can be pruned to expose trunks.

When to prune   Late dormant season for major cuts; after spring growth to shape.

Pruning Fruit Trees, Bushes, and Vines

Pruning and training that begin at planting time mean trees bear better-quality fruit at a younger age and produce greater yields. Yearly pruning keeps fruit-bearing wood productive and plants healthy and vigorous.

In order to grow good quality fruit, you must prune. No other woody plants are as dependent upon thoughtful and consistent pruning as are fruit trees, bushes, and vines. The pruning and training systems described here are designed to expose foliage and fruit-bearing stems to maximum sunlight, the key to producing large sweet fruit and a top-quality harvest.

Fruiting plants must be pruned from the time they are planted to help them develop a strong, well-balanced framework of branches. This is easily done with hand pruners and takes little time; if pruning is delayed until a tree is larger, the task requires more time and tools. Without early training fruit trees develop branches that shade one another and produce poor quality fruit. With proper pruning the plants may take several more years to bear fruit than they would have if not trained while young, but fruit quality is far superior.

After the basic branching structure of a young plant is established, pruning is required every year to remove unproductive branches, limit size, and increase the amount of light that reaches the remaining limbs. This increases productivity and allows the fruit to ripen with better color; spraying to control pests and diseases can also be carried out more easily and effectively.

Apple trees should be pruned in late winter when the branches are easy to see. Late winter is also the time of year when pruning cuts heal fastest.

PRUNING FRUIT TREES

Any area of a fruit tree that receives less than 30 percent full sun will bear a reduced crop of smaller fruit of poor quality and color. By pruning to restrict the height and spread of the tree, you can prevent branches and foliage from shading the interior; the result will be a large crop of more appealing fruit. When a fruit tree begins to bear heavily, growth slows and so does the need for pruning.

Three pruning systems that change the shape and branching structure of the tree are commonly used for fruit trees. The central-leader system emphasizes one tall main trunk with tiers of branches arising from it; the vase or open-center system features a short trunk about 3 feet tall and an open center consisting of three or four main branches; the modified central-leader system, a compromise between the central-leader and the vase systems, features a short trunk and several tiers of branches. Although any type of fruit tree can be pruned according to any of these systems, most types respond best to a particular system. In this chapter the most suitable method is described for each type of fruit tree.

How Fruit Trees Grow

Fruit trees respond just as landscape plants to thinning and heading cuts (see the chapter "Pruning Techniques," page 5). Apical dominance dictates the pattern of growth and branching. Avoid excessive pruning that unnecessarily removes food-producing leaves. Mature trees tolerate more pruning than do younger trees. Older trees respond best to

This 'Red Delicious' apple tree bears a heavy crop because its branches have been trained to a 90-degree angle to the trunk, encouraging the growth of fruit-bearing wood.

Fruit Tree Training Methods

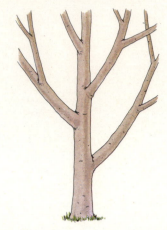

Central leader: With one main trunk, this shape can hold a heavy crop of fruit and resist storm damage.

Vase: The vase or open-center pruning method allows plenty of light and air into the tree's interior, encouraging fruit production on lower branches.

Modified central leader: A compromise between the vase and the central leader shapes, the tree with a modified central leader has both strength and a sunny center.

Water Sprout Removal

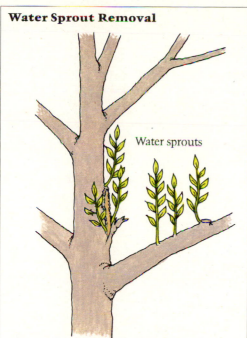

Water sprouts

The rapidly growing, soft shoots that grow upright from main branches are called water sprouts. They commonly appear after heavy pruning, but will not fruit well and are susceptible to insect attack. Remove water sprouts as soon as they appear.

thinning, in which relatively large branches rather than many small ones are removed. Prune young trees only enough to develop a desirable scaffold branch system because needless pruning delays fruit production.

Fruit trees may produce vertical branches that grow vigorously upward at the expense of fruit-bearing wood. Encourage wide-spreading branches because such branches produce especially well and have a more desirable balance between vegetative and fruiting wood. By using wooden or metal spreaders between the trunk and scaffold branches on young apple and pear trees, it is possible to change the position of unfruitful upright lateral branches and make them more productive. Spreading the branches reduces the rate of growth and increases the formation of flowering and fruiting wood. Using spreaders encourages fruit production in a fast-growing, lightly fruiting tree.

When to Prune

Fruit trees and ornamental landscape plants in general benefit from pruning during the late dormant season before the start of new

Parts of a Fruit Tree Branch

Terminal bud: The fat bud at the branch tip grows the fastest. Remove it and several buds will break dormancy behind it.

Leaf bud: Flat triangular buds on the sides of a branch will form leaves. To make one grow, cut off the stem just above it.

Flower bud: Plump buds on branches will form flowers; they are the first buds to swell in spring. On stone fruits they grow alone or beside leaf buds. On apples and pears, flower buds contain a few leaves.

Spurs: The squat twiglets tipped with fat flower buds that grow on older branches of apples, pears, plums, and apricots are spurs. These produce flowers and then fruit; don't remove them.

Bud scar: A ring on a branch that marks the point where a terminal bud began growing after the dormant season. This line marks the beginning of the present season's growth.

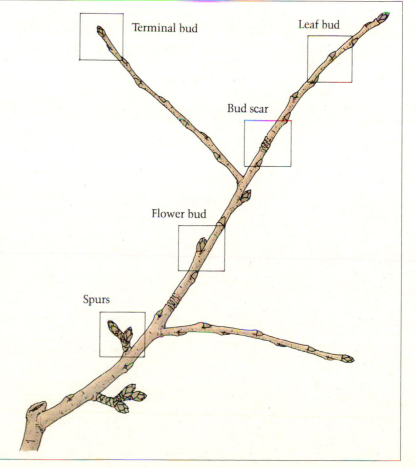

Terminal bud

Leaf bud

Bud scar

Flower bud

Spurs

Fruit Tree Pruning Basics

A tree's response to a pruning cut depends upon where the cut was made. Both heading and thinning cuts are used in pruning fruit trees and grapes.

Heading cuts

Make a slanting cut just beyond a bud.

Several buds left on the cut branch grow, resulting in denser, more compact foliage on more branches.

Thinning cuts

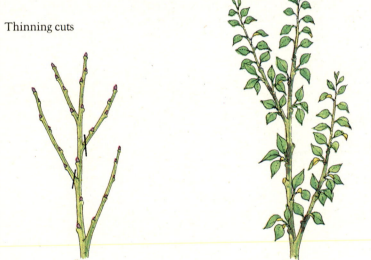

Branches are removed entirely at their origins. The tree's energy is diverted into the remaining branches, which grow more vigorously.

late fall or early winter may predispose the tree to injury from the cold winter temperatures that follow.

Under certain conditions, fruit trees can be pruned during the summer. Pruning in early summer promotes fruit set as well as unwanted vegetative growth. New growth resulting from heading cuts on one-year-old wood is especially lush and damaging to the training program. To avoid unwanted new shoots, thin to a spur on two- or three-year-old wood.

Prune from early to mid-August to dwarf a too-vigorous tree. Do not, however, prune trees less than three years old during summer since pruning at this time could limit their growth. Late-summer pruning, which promotes minimal new growth, has the least harmful effect on flowering and fruit set the next year. Late-summer removal of foliage that would have shaded the maturing fruit may even improve fruit color.

It's a good policy to limit summer pruning to 10 to 20 cuts on a six- to eight-year-old tree. In general, excessive summer pruning simply results in smaller fruit of poorer quality.

Pruning Cuts

Thinning cuts, as described in "Pruning Techniques," page 5, and "Pruning Deciduous Trees," page 21, are the primary pruning techniques. Thinning removes selected branches without disrupting the existing growth pattern. Every thinning cut increases sunlight penetration to the tree's interior and promotes greater flowering and better-quality fruit. Cut a branch or shoot back to the parent stem without leaving a stub. To shorten long branches prune to a side branch with a diameter no less than one third smaller; it will assume apical dominance.

Heading cuts, which encourage new growth directly behind the pruning cut, are sometimes used to advantage on fruit trees. Use a heading cut to induce side branches on apple varieties that don't branch adequately—for example, 'Tydeman's Red', spur-type 'Delicious', and 'Rome Beauty'. Heading cuts can also be used to stiffen primary scaffold branches; heading the branch stops the terminal growth and directs energy into thickening the scaffold. A branch can also be headed to shorten it and keep it in balance with the other scaffolds.

growth. This is the best time to determine which branches need pruning. In addition, the tissue loss at this time is least damaging to the plant. Pruning can be delayed, however, as much as a week after flowering with minimal harm to the plant.

Woody plants store food reserves, carbohydrates primarily, in their branches during the winter. Although all pruning dwarfs a plant to some extent because it removes these stored food reserves, late dormant-season pruning has the least harmful effect. Removing active foliage during summer and fall may rob the tree of energy it needs to close wounds, develop fruit buds, and extend new shoots. Pruning in

APPLE TREES

Almost all apple trees are grafted. The mature height of the tree depends on the type of rootstock to which it is grafted. Standard trees, which can exceed 20 feet tall, are grown on normal apple seedling rootstocks. Dwarf and semidwarf trees are grafted onto dwarfing rootstocks, which slow the growth of the trunk and branches. Genetic dwarf trees are naturally dwarf no matter which kind of rootstock they grow on. Although all apple trees bear fruit on short shoots called spurs, some trees are called spur-types. These are mutations of standard apple trees that produce more fruiting spurs than do standards. Spur-type trees remain 30 percent smaller than non-spur strains grafted onto similar rootstocks.

Central-Leader Training

There are several different pruning methods used for apples: central-leader training, modified central-leader training, and vase training. The choice depends upon the size of the tree. In home gardens, the central-leader system is most often used because it is suitable for dwarf and semidwarf trees, which are usually planted in home orchards. This system trains apple trees into a pyramidal shape to maximize vital sunlight exposure.

First year Begin training as soon as the new tree is planted; this should be done during the dormant season. If starting with an unbranched nursery tree, called a whip, head the tree to 24 to 28 inches above the ground; do this regardless of the type of apple tree or rootstock. The first group of scaffold branches will be among the new sprouts generated below the cut. In the early summer select one shoot to be the leader and four others spaced evenly around the trunk to be the lower scaffolds. Remove all other shoots. On spur-type trees, five main scaffolds can be selected.

If beginning with a branched tree, remove any laterals on the lower 18 inches of the trunk. From the remaining branches select a central leader and four laterals that are evenly spaced around the stem; remove all others. Cut back long laterals by one third to one half and head the leader to 12 inches above the topmost lateral. If the tree has weak or broken branches, remove all laterals and treat it as a one-year-old whip.

When properly pruned, apple trees bear fruit at an early age, but if left to grow without guidance, fruit bearing may be delayed by several years.

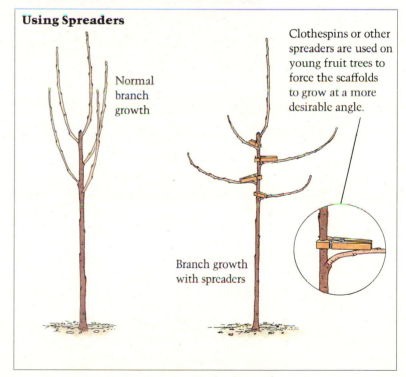

Using Spreaders

Normal branch growth

Branch growth with spreaders

Clothespins or other spreaders are used on young fruit trees to force the scaffolds to grow at a more desirable angle.

Some of the shoots that develop in response to the pruning cuts may have narrow crotch angles. Correct this weakness and develop them into strong scaffolds by forcing them to grow at a wider angle. Spreading these young green shoots to a wide angle increases fruiting, slows growth by 10 to 15 percent, establishes dominance of the central leader, and increases structural strength in the scaffold

Branch Angles

Vigorous tip growth

No flower buds

30°

Without a spreader, the scaffold forms a narrow angle that is weakly attached and produces tip and foliage growth at the expense of flowers and fruit.

Spreader

Moderate tip growth

Flower buds

60°

When branches are spread to a desirable angle, tip growth slows and flower buds form and produce plenty of fruit.

Spreader

Water sprouts

Little tip growth

90°

If branches are spread too far, tip growth is minimal and unproductive water sprouts form at the expense of flowers and fruit.

branches. Wider crotch angles are also more resistant to winter injuries, which tend to occur at narrow angles. Spreading shoots too far results in unproductive upright suckers along the lengths of the shoots. A scaffold growing at a 60-degree angle generally forms the most fruiting spurs and is highly productive.

Force the short flexible stems away from the trunk with toothpicks, wire spreaders, or clothespins. Spread them to a 90-degree angle from the trunk while the flexible shoots are 3 to 6 inches long and green at the base. After about four weeks remove the spreaders. Although shoots are initially spread to 90 degrees, as they grow they assume a more desirable 60-degree angle.

Retain most of the foliage during the first year to encourage growth of a large root system. Save further pruning for the next dormant season, early the next spring.

Second year   One year after planting head the leader to 24 to 30 inches above the topmost scaffold branch. Do this during dormancy. This cut encourages the growth of shoots that will form the second tier of scaffold branches. If laterals have already formed at approximately this height, keep them as long as they are less vigorous than the scaffolds below. Head the leader in either event.

Continue to remove shoots on the lower 18 inches of trunk, as well as any stems that develop higher on the trunk and compete with the four first-year scaffolds. Cut off any branches that grow between the first and second tiers. Don't head the older scaffolds on nonspur-type trees after the second growing season. Spur-type trees may benefit from heading, but only if done two weeks after full bloom, the best time for encouraging more shoots to grow.

To develop a productive second tier of scaffolds, insert spreaders as for the first tier. If the crotch angle of the first tier is less than 60 degrees when new growth begins, then use longer wooden or metal spreaders to force branches to the proper angle. Don't let the angle become greater than 60 degrees or unproductive water sprouts may arise. The spreaders can be removed in midsummer because the new wood produced will hold the branch at the altered angle. If the angle is still not wide enough, repeat the procedure the next year.

Left: Because of its compact size, a dwarf apple tree is easy to prune, spray, and harvest. And it can fit into most home landscapes.
Right: Pears, such as this 'Bartlett', can grow tall and are often pruned to maintain a central leader.

Spreading the branches does not damage the tree. However, if the central leader appears weak and bends when the spreaders are inserted, wait until the next year. After the fourth year, a branch loses some flexibility and must be tied down with rope or twine and weights to encourage spreading.

Third year From the third year on, the pruning goals are to develop the central leader and to train the third and fourth tiers of scaffolds. Just as in the previous years, cut the leader to 24 to 30 inches above the second tier or use existing branches if they are appropriately placed. Maintain a pyramidal shape by leaving the lower scaffolds long and thinning those above to lateral side branches. Remove rapidly growing branches at the top of the tree but keep any that are slower growing; they will be at a wider angle of emergence and will fruit more readily.

Thin unwanted branches by cutting them back to the scaffolds. Cut back any upright branches emerging from the scaffolds to a downward-growing shoot. Pull off water sprouts by hand when they are 6 to 10 inches long. This also removes latent buds at the base of the sprout. Removing water sprouts early reduces infestations of aphids, which are attracted to the soft growth.

Later years The central-leader system produces the best fruit color, quality, and size of any training method. It maximizes sunlight penetration throughout the tree. Although a mature tree can easily be maintained at the desired height and spread, it will be necessary to prune regularly to restrict top growth. If top pruning is neglected, the vigorous upright shoots, which receive maximum sunlight, will grow faster than those below and distort the productive conical shape.

When the tree reaches a convenient height for harvesting and spraying, restrict further growth but still maintain the tree's vigor. Each year during the dormant season cut all one-year-old laterals off the central leader. Then head the leader by one half of the previous year's growth. Apical dominance will be restored below the cut and then new, upright-growing shoots will form from the dormant or adventitious buds. Remove any water sprouts and suckers.

As the tree matures it will be necessary to thin limbs to allow sunlight to penetrate throughout the tree. If the top tiers become overgrown with large branches, remove them rather than prune a large quantity of smaller branches. This measure temporarily limits yields on the upper scaffolds but the lower tier becomes more productive.

PEAR TREES

The central-leader system is recommended for pear trees as well as for apples. Proceed in much the same manner, bearing in mind certain characteristics of pears.

Pear trees are highly susceptible to fire blight, a bacterial disease that infects the tree through both the flowers and the shoot tips. Fast-growing water sprouts and terminals are especially vulnerable, so keep pruning to a minimum; this applies especially to any heading cuts, which stimulate susceptible new growth. Once the central-leader framework is established, remove only small branches, water sprouts, or limbs that rub. If the tree grows too tall, thin back the branch tips to small laterals to discourage the growth of disease-susceptible soft new shoots.

As with apples, prune pears lightly every year once the central-leader framework is established. Be sure to remove branches or terminals killed by fire blight to prevent the disease from spreading. Infected branches can be identified by their scorched-looking leaves. Cut off twigs and branches with black and sunken cankers, making cuts 4 to 6 inches beyond the visible damage to prevent further spread of the disease.

Pruning Peaches and Nectarines

All fruit forms on wood that grew during the previous season. Long branches are more productive than short ones. Prune off about half the new growth each spring, removing short branches entirely and heading long branches by a third. This encourages abundant new growth for a good crop the next year. Cut out tangled center growth for more light penetration.

Last year's growth now bearing fruit

This year's growth now forming next year's buds

PEACH AND NECTARINE TREES

Since a completely satisfactory dwarfing rootstock for peaches and nectarines has yet to be found, these trees grow on their own rootstocks; they usually grow 15 feet tall and wide, but can be kept smaller. The pruning instructions described here apply to these standard-sized trees. Genetic or natural dwarf peach and nectarine plants grow in bush form and require very little pruning.

Open-Center or Vase Training

The open-center pruning method, suitable for all fruit trees including standard-sized apples, is most successful for peaches and nectarines. This method produces a vase-shaped tree, consisting of a framework of three or four scaffolds of equal lengths and no central leader.

When training peach and nectarine trees, remember that they are prone to cold-weather damage. Wait to prune them until the late dormant season, when it is easier to detect branches and flower buds that have been winter-killed. If a flower bud looks as if it has been winter-killed, cut it in half; an injured bud will have a dark center. Winter-killed stems look wrinkled and the wood beneath the bark is brown; the inner bark of live stems is a healthy green.

First year Begin pruning at planting time by cutting a one-year-old peach or nectarine whip back to 24 to 28 inches above the ground. If one or two suitable branches remain 2 to 4 inches below the cut, head them back to two or three buds and keep them as scaffolds. Remove all other growth.

Two or three months later, dormant buds just below the cut will have grown into small shoots. Select the shoots that emerge at a wide angle from the trunk for the primary scaffolds. Peach and nectarine trees are hardier when all scaffolds have wide angles of attachment. If none of the uppermost shoots has a promising angle, pinch shoots back to 2 to 3 inches long to force the development of less vigorous shoots or dormant buds lower on the branch. These usually have wide emergence angles. If the tree has only one or two suitable primary scaffolds, head these to stubs a few inches long to force the growth of other potential scaffolds.

Training for a Vase Shape

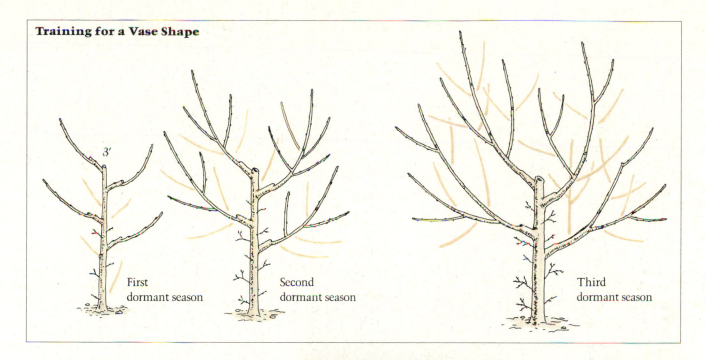

First
dormant season

Second
dormant season

Third
dormant season

Remove any shoots below the lowest existing scaffold. If one scaffold grows faster than the others, shorten it by thinning to an outward-growing shoot so that all are equal in length. Three to five weeks later, shorten any excessively vigorous laterals again and select any scaffolds still needed.

Second year   In the second dormant season, continue developing the open center of the tree. Cut back upward-growing branches near the center of the tree to short stubs. The small cluster of growth that develops from these stubs helps keep the center open for the next few months.

Remove any growth that has developed below the primary scaffolds and any shoots that arise on the scaffolds within 6 inches of the trunk. If the three or four primary scaffolds have not yet been selected, make the selection now. Continue to cut fast-growing branches to the length of the others by pruning to an outward-growing lateral.

In mid-spring, cut back the stubby center growth again to maintain the open center and, once again, equalize the height of the scaffolds. Finally, remove any shoots growing on the trunk below the lowest scaffold. Maintaining an open center directs dominant growth to the scaffolds.

Third year   By this time, primary scaffold branches will have been chosen and all of the

competing branches removed. When the tree is dormant, eliminate branches with narrow-angled crotches or limbs that are crossing or growing into the center. If the stubby center shoots have not been shaded by the scaffolds, remove them. Maintain a well-balanced shape by thinning each scaffold to an outward-growing shoot approximately at the same height.

At the end of this season, the form of the tree should be clearly recognizable.

Peach trees bear fruit on one-year-old wood and require heavy annual pruning to stimulate new growth. They are often pruned into a vase shape to allow plenty of growth-stimulating light into the interior of the tree.

A Japanese plum tree pruned into a vase shape doubles as a landscape subject.

Pruning Apricots and Japanese Plums

Cut ½ of new wood

Spurs (fruit grows here)

Last season's branch

Most fruit is formed on short spurs growing on two- or three-year-old wood. Each year, head back the previous year's growth by half; the half left will form fruit spurs the following summer and produce a good crop of fruit the year after that.

Fruit-Bearing Trees

When peach and nectarine trees are large enough to bear fruit, the pruning objective is to encourage abundant growth of good fruit-bearing stems and to thin branches so light can penetrate throughout the tree. These trees bear flower buds on one-year-old terminal growth; the best shoots for fruit production are 6 to 18 inches long. Remove weaker or very vigorous shoots.

Begin in the dormant season by thinning back the primary branches to outward-growing laterals. To keep the center open, remove inward-growing shoots. Carefully thin small lateral branches along the entire length of each scaffold, leaving fruiting shoots that are the optimum length. Next remove diseased, damaged, downward-growing, rubbing, or crossing branches.

Maintain the tree height at 6 to 8 feet for easy harvesting. Cut upward-growing branches to strong outward-growing laterals, preferably by standing on the ground and using lopping shears or a pole pruner. Pruning from the ground helps keep the tree conveniently short.

Every year prune the scaffolds back to the same height to limit size and develop new fruiting wood. Since apical dominance is lost, several lateral stems will arise close to the pruning cuts. Retain some of the new growth for the following season's fruiting wood and thin the lesser shoots. In future years make cuts to outward-growing laterals just above or below the previous years' cuts.

PLUM TREES

The Japanese plum cultivars, which form naturally spreading trees, respond quite well to the open-center pruning method, described for peach and nectarine trees. Not as many heading cuts are required on a plum tree; instead concentrate on thinning small twigs and branches to increase fruit size on young trees.

The central-leader system used for apples is best for European plum cultivars. Keep the spacing between sets of scaffolds about 18 inches. As fruit bearing begins, thin some growth to maintain fruiting in the lower parts of the tree.

APRICOT TREES

Apricots may be pruned by either the open-center method, as described for peaches and nectarines, or the modified central-leader, as described below for cherries. Since apricots bloom very early and the flowers or fruit often are frost damaged, wait to prune until after flowering. As with peaches and nectarines, cut back long branches to an outward-growing lateral branch. Thin to keep the interior open to sunlight.

Since they bear fruit on new wood, apricots need to be pruned every year to be fruitful. Pruning encourages new stems to develop and grow to about 18 to 24 inches long; these branches flower and fruit the following year.

CHERRY TREES

Although the open-center pruning described for peaches and nectarines is suitable for both sweet and sour cherries, the modified central-leader method has become the method of choice for both types of cherries.

Sour Cherry Trees

Begin pruning after planting a well-branched whip. Remove all branches except three or four that emerge in different directions and are separated vertically by 6 to 8 inches. The first branch should be no lower than 18 to 24 inches from the ground. Select and encourage a central leader by removing any competing branches.

During the following two to four years, develop a second tier of laterals. Select two or three promising branches 18 inches above the lower set; then remove the leader. Use spreaders to widen narrow crotches if necessary (see pages 93 and 94).

Now that the branching framework has been established, the only pruning needed is to maintain the basic scaffold branches. This may include thinning some growth to sustain viable fruiting wood in the interior of the tree.

Sweet Cherry Trees

As with sour cherries select scaffold branches that emerge at wide angles. Since these trees can become large, prune long branches to outward-growing laterals to maintain a convenient height. This also keeps the center open and allows light to penetrate to the fruiting wood on the interior of the tree.

CITRUS TREES

Citrus trees don't require major structural pruning. There is no need to prune a citrus tree unless a branch is about to break. Lemon trees, for example, tend to set fruit at the tips of thin branches; this may overload and break them. To correct this tendency cut all laterals in half and pinch back new growth several times during the season.

Cherry trees produce a cloud of white blossoms in early spring. Pruning is best accomplished before leaves emerge.

Pruning Citrus

Pinch

Cut

Prune citrus only if the fruit crop is so heavy it may break a branch.

To correct, cut side branches back by half and then pinch new growth several times during the summer.

OVERGROWN FRUIT TREES

When pruning is neglected, it doesn't take long for fruit trees to become overgrown. The outer branches become dense and eventually shade the inner branches, limiting fruit yields. To bring these neglected trees back to full production, it is necessary to reduce their height, spread, and denseness.

First thin undesirable interior branches that cross or crowd other branches. Generally it's better to eliminate all of these branches at one time unless there are more than four large branches to cut. If so, remove them gradually over two years. Prune off downward-growing, broken, diseased, or dead branches.

To reduce tree height cut upward-growing branches off at an outward-growing branch that is nearly the same diameter and about the height desired for the tree. On severely overgrown trees that are much taller than desired, make no more than three or four of these cuts each year until the height is sufficiently reduced. Gradually lowering the tree minimizes the excessive water sprout growth that often follows a significant reduction in tree height.

Continue to thin remaining branches throughout the tree, targeting weak growth, water sprouts, and underhanging branches. Begin thinning at the periphery of the tree and work back toward the trunk, leaving some fruit-bearing wood in the interior.

FRUIT THINNING

When fruit trees set too much fruit in one year, the stress can reduce the size of the following year's crop. Thin young fruit to prevent future crop loss, especially in apples. Because fruit trees initiate flower buds for the following season only four to six weeks after full bloom, try to thin fruit no later than 50 days after full bloom. Pruning delayed until midsummer cannot influence next year's crop, but it can improve the size, color, and shape of the current season's fruit.

Pull excess fruit off by hand when it is ¾ inch in diameter. You can follow up and thin again several weeks later, this time removing the smallest fruit to allow more energy to be channeled into the larger fruit. Be careful not to injure the flowering spurs on apples and other fruit trees; leave the fruit stem attached to the spur or branch to prevent injury. Hold

Rejuvenating a Neglected Apple Tree

Before pruning

After pruning

the stem between your thumb and forefinger and push the fruit off the stem with the remaining fingers. Leave one fruit per cluster and space these several inches apart. Apples should be spaced 6 inches apart; peaches and nectarines thinned to 4 to 6 inches apart; apricots and plums to 2 to 3 inches apart. Cherries and pears do not need thinning.

Fruit Thinning

Apricots

Plums

Nectarines

Peaches

Apples

FRUITING BUSHES AND VINES

Most small fruits including strawberries, raspberries, blackberries, gooseberries, currants, blueberries, and grapes require pruning or training to encourage them to produce well.

STRAWBERRIES

The first year strawberries are planted should be dedicated to root growth; this develops a solid foundation for good productivity in years to come. During the first growing season, remove blossoms of June-bearing varieties as soon as they appear. Remove blossoms of everbearing types up until midsummer of the first year; a small crop of berries may develop later in the summer from subsequent flowers.

Strawberry plants form horizontal stems, called runners, with small plants at the tip. In the fall both the parent plant and the plantlets set flower buds, which bloom and bear fruit the following summer. Pinch runners to control both size and quantity of strawberries. Removing all runners produces a big plant with less but larger fruit. Allowing the runners to root and fruit produces a larger harvest but smaller strawberries. Choose one of the two systems of growing strawberries or keep a few runners and pinch off the others.

After the last berries of June-bearers are gone in midsummer, shear the foliage with a rotary lawn mower 1 to 2 inches above the crown to encourage new growth. Renew beds by thinning weak plants and leaving the strong ones spaced 6 to 8 inches apart. Then till a strip of fresh soil 12 to 18 inches wide between rows. This annual task, combined with proper fertilizing, watering and pest control, makes a strawberry planting productive for two to four years. When yields decline, remove old plants, improve the soil, and begin anew with fresh plants.

BLACK AND PURPLE RASPBERRIES

Each type of bramble has a unique growth pattern that needs different pruning techniques. To understand how to prune brambles such as raspberries and blackberries, you must first realize that these are biennial producers. Each spring new shoots arise from the crown but they do not flower or bear fruit until the second year. Cut these canes back to

the base when they die after fruiting. Unpruned plants develop into a thicket that gives the name bramble true meaning.

There is an exception to this life cycle. Canes of everbearing brambles produce a crop late in the first summer and repeat with another crop in midsummer of the second year before they die.

Plant black and purple raspberries with one plant per hill. Thin all but seven or eight of the strongest and thickest stems as the new plants grow. Either after harvest or the following spring, prune off close to the ground those canes that have borne fruit. If waiting until spring, prune before the buds begin to swell but after danger of frost has passed.

In the summer top the first-year canes to encourage a strong plant with fruitful side branches. Top new canes of black raspberries when they reach 24 inches tall by cutting or snapping off the top 2 to 4 inches of growth. Do the same to purple raspberries when the canes approach 30 inches tall.

During the following dormant season, cut back the side branches on new fruiting canes

Above: Strawberries produce the largest berries when their runners are continually removed; if the runners are allowed to spread, more fruit develops but berries are small. Opposite: Raspberries and other brambles produce flowers and fruit only on one-year-old wood. They need yearly pruning to remove old canes and make room for new flowering wood.

to increase berry size. On black raspberries shorten the laterals until they contain 8 to 12 buds or are 6 to 10 inches long. Prune purple raspberries, which are more vigorous, back to 11 to 16 buds. Then cut back any spindly or short laterals. Ideally the plant should have four to five strong fruiting canes remaining.

RED RASPBERRIES

Use the same procedures described for black and purple raspberries for red raspberries, but eliminate the summer topping. Topping reduces yields of red raspberries. These raspberries normally don't produce any side branches because the canes aren't topped to encourage branching.

Grow red raspberries in a hedgerow and don't let the row spread wider than 18 inches. Thin individual canes by cutting them at ground level so they are spaced 6 to 10 inches apart. Leave the largest diameter canes, which are the most productive. After the harvest remove canes that have borne fruit. During the dormant season, head back canes growing within a wire support by one quarter of their length. If there is no support, keep the canes at about 3 feet tall.

Treat everbearing cultivars similarly, but leave the first-year canes that have just fruited intact in the fall. They will fruit again in summer, after which they can be removed.

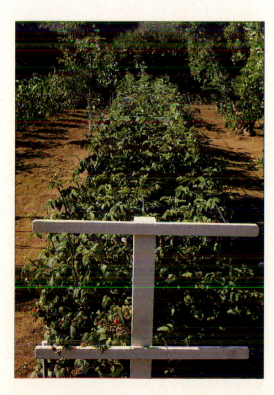

Pruning Rigid and Trailing Blackberries and Raspberries

Last year's growth is blooming and bearing fruit as new shoots emerge from the crown. Remove all but 5 of these new shoots and let them continue to grow on the ground.

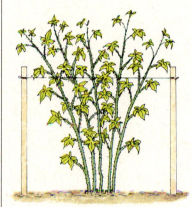

After harvest, cut all the bearing canes to the ground and tie the 5 new canes to the wire.

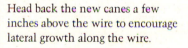

Head back the new canes a few inches above the wire to encourage lateral growth along the wire.

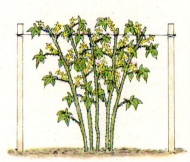

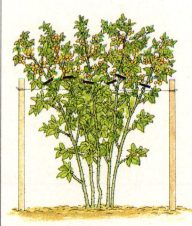

After the fall harvest of red and yellow raspberries on these new canes, cut back the portion that fruited.

In winter, cut the laterals back to 18". They will bear during the coming summer and continue the cycle.

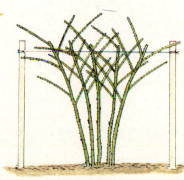

Training Rigid Berries on a Double Wire

Rather than being grown in a row, rigid blackberries or raspberries can be trained to grow on a double wire to keep their stems under control. After fruiting, remove old canes and tie up the new ones.

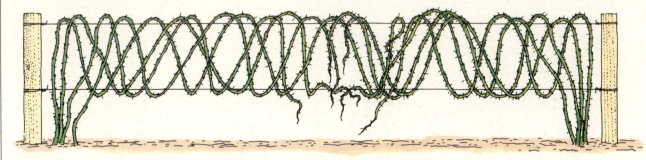

Training Trailing Berries on a Single Wire

An alternate method to the hedgerow is growing trailing raspberries and blackberries on a single wire. Wrap the stems around the wire and do not prune. After harvest, cut off old canes and tie up the new ones.

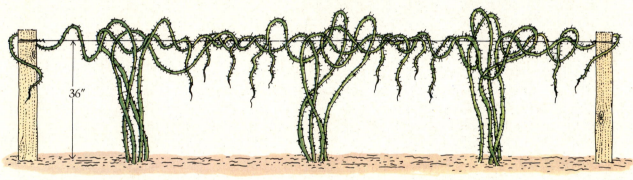

36"

BLACKBERRIES

When planting blackberries in a hedgerow, restrict upright cultivars to three or four canes per plant and cut or pull out the rest. Allow 12 to 18 shoots per foot with trailing types. Prune blackberries the same as black raspberries with one exception: Leave laterals on second-year canes 12 to 18 inches long.

Thin trailing blackberries to seven or eight canes per plant by removing unwanted canes at ground level. Shorten the canes to about 5 feet long and tie them all to a stake or trellis. Omit the summer topping. On upright-growing blackberries top new shoots back to 30 to 36 inches. Cut or pull out excess sucker shoots during the summer or the plant will develop into an unruly thicket.

BOYSENBERRIES AND LOGANBERRIES

Like the other bramble fruits, these berries are biennial and require annual pruning. Support the canes on a 36-inch-high wire stretched between two poles. In spring thin all but five of the first-year canes and remove the old fruiting canes. Let the new canes grow on the ground until they exceed 36 inches. Then tie them to the support and head them just above the wire to encourage strong lateral branches. The following spring cut the laterals to 18 inches; they will fruit later in the summer. Remove fruiting canes at ground level after harvest.

BLUEBERRIES

Wait to prune young blueberry bushes until their fourth year. Then during the early spring dormant season remove dead, weak, or short terminal stems, as well as any crossing branches that block light from the interior.

Blueberries form flower buds on strong one-year-old wood; plants that don't have vigorous new wood should be pruned to encourage new growth. On mature plants it may be necessary to thin older branches that have the most fine twiggy growth and the fewest strong one-year-old shoots. Cut them at the crown to encourage new growth. Head small branches with small flower buds.

Pruning Blueberries

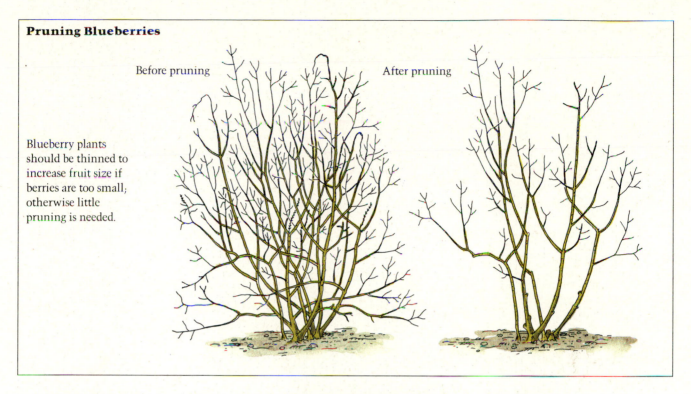

Before pruning

After pruning

Blueberry plants should be thinned to increase fruit size if berries are too small; otherwise little pruning is needed.

Judge the amount of thinning needed by the size of the berries. If they have been small, prune more heavily the following dormant season. If large, limit pruning.

GOOSEBERRIES

Unlike most other small fruits, gooseberries bear fruit on first-year wood as well as on spurs of older wood. They tend to overbear and are susceptible to mildew—two problems pruning can help control.

Gooseberries start producing the second season after planting but maximum harvest begins the fourth season if the shrub is pruned properly. After planting cut out all but six shoots to form an open, vase-shaped plant. Remove any stems that touch the ground, both now and later in the season. This maximizes air circulation and sunlight penetration and discourages mildew.

During the third and fourth dormant seasons, remove the weakest old wood to encourage new, more productive branches. After the fourth year cut out all three-year-old wood entirely because it will no longer bear fruit. Thin some first- and second-year canes as well.

If this pruning does not stimulate growth of renewal shoots, head third-year wood to stubs 4 to 6 inches long. Limit the resulting new growth to about six canes.

CURRANTS AND ELDERBERRIES

Naturally full and shrubby plants, currants fruit best if plants are pruned to six to eight stems. Although they will produce on older wood, currants bear fruit best on two- and three-year-old stems. Start pruning currants during the second season by removing dead, small, and broken branches. The following years thin three- and four-year-old wood during the dormant season.

Elderberries grow in much the same fashion as currants except they spread considerably more. Limit new shoots to a circle 2 feet wide around the original plant.

GRAPE VINES

Grape vines must be pruned heavily to bear good crops. For the first three years after planting, cut off all but six to eight bunches of immature grapes so that energy can go toward strengthening the root system. From the fourth year on, leave half of the bunches on the vine. Training begins at two years but the method varies depending upon the grape variety.

Four-Armed Kniffin System

The four-armed Kniffin system, the easiest for home gardeners, is suitable for *Vitus vinifera* and for most American grapes including 'Concord' and 'Delaware'.

Training Spur and Cane Grapes for the First Three Seasons

When planting: Plant a rooted cutting with 2 or 3 buds left above the soil; then bury in light mulch.

First growing season: The plant will grow a number of shoots; leave these alone.

First dormant season: Choose the best shoot and cut all the others to their bases. Head the remaining shoot to 3 or 4 strong buds.

Second growing season: When new shoots reach about 12" long, select the most vigorous and pinch others off at the trunk. Tie the remaining shoot to a support (arbor or trellis post). When the shoot reaches the arbor top or trellis wire, pinch it to force branching. Let 2 strong branches grow. Pinch any others at 8" to 10" long.

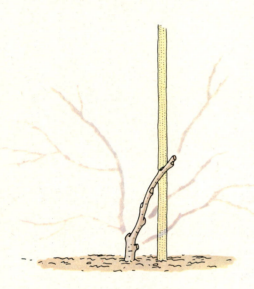

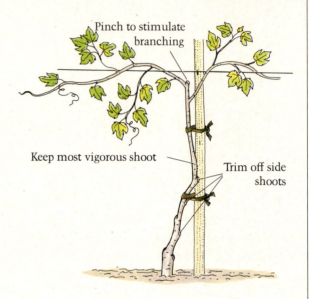

Pinch to stimulate branching

Keep most vigorous shoot

Trim off side shoots

Second dormant season: Cut away side shoots, leaving only the trunk and 2 major branches. Tie these to the arbor top or the trellis wire.

Third growing season: Let the vine grow. Pinch tips of sprouts on trunk. After this, spur and cane pruning differ.

Trim all other growth

Pinch

Spur Training of Grapes After Third Growing Season

Third dormant season: Remove the weakest shoots along the horizontal branches at their bases, choosing the strongest side shoots spaced 6'' to 10'' apart. Cut these to 2 buds. Remove all shoots from the vertical trunk.

Annually: Every dormant season after this, each spur will have 2 shoots that fruited during the summer. Cut the strongest spurs to 2 or 3 buds; these will produce fruit-bearing shoots in summer. Remove any weak spurs. Keep the trunk free of growth. Repeat pruning procedure each year.

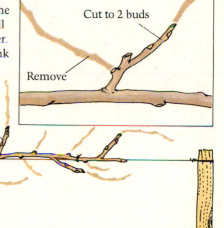

Cut to 2 buds

Remove

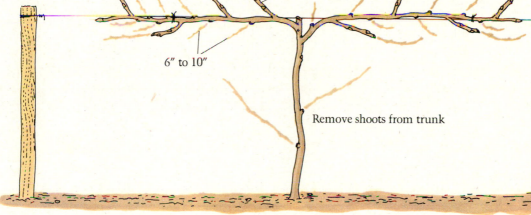

Cut strongest spurs to 2 buds

6" to 10"

Remove shoots from trunk

Cane Training of Grapes After Third Growing Season

Third dormant season: Remove shoots from the trunk. Cut the horizontal branches back so that 2 long shoots remain on each. (On a double-wire trellis you can leave up to 8 shoots per vine.) Tie the shoot farthest from the trunk to the trellis. Cut the other back to 2 or 3 buds. The tied shoot will produce fruit in the summer; the cut shoot will produce growth for replacing the tied shoot.

Annually: During dormancy, cut back the tied cane, which bore fruit, to its base. The other cane will have grown 2 or 3 new long shoots. Select the best and tie it to the trellis; it will bear fruit in summer. Cut the next best cane to 2 or 3 buds. Remove the weakest at its base. Remove any growth from the trunk. Repeat each dormant season.

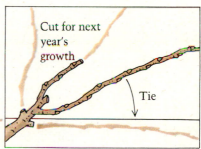

Cut for next year's growth

Tie

Cut renewal spur to 2 or 3 buds

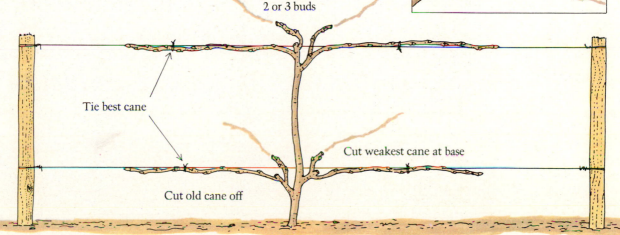

Tie best cane

Cut weakest cane at base

Cut old cane off

Begin by tying a young vine to a stake to develop a permanent trunk. Stretch two wires, one 30 to 36 inches high and the other 54 to 60 inches high, between posts spaced 5 to 6 feet on each side of the plant. As the vine grows tie it to the wires. When it passes the first wire, pinch off all lower side shoots. Pinch the tip when it extends 1 foot beyond the top wire.

Just prior to the start of growth during the second year, cut the trunk back, severing a bud located just above the top wire. To develop the four arms, remove all side shoots except for one on each side of both wires. Cut these shoots back to two buds. Secure the lateral branches that grow from these buds to the wires.

During the third late-winter pruning season, cut off all but four shoots on each lateral branch. Two shoots will be fruiting canes. Prune them back to 10 buds. Prune back the other two canes more severely to two buds; these will be the renewal spurs that bear fruit during the following year.

The fourth winter and every following year, cut off the two long canes that have borne fruit. The four remaining spurs will have sent out several shoots the previous year. Prune the upper shoots into fruiting canes with 10 buds each and keep the lower shoots as renewal spurs with 2 buds.

Spur Pruning

Spur-pruning is suitable for most European grape varieties including 'Tokay', 'Muscat', and 'Malaga', as well as for the California grape varieties. The exception is 'Thompson Seedless', which should be grown by the four-armed Kniffin system.

During the second summer after planting, stretch a wire 30 inches high between two supports on either side of the vine. When the vine climbs about 1 foot above the wire, cut it back so that it is even with the wire. When the top two buds grow, train one along the wire in one direction, the other in the opposite direction. Tie each shoot loosely to the wire.

During the second winter cut off all lateral growth from the two branches, being careful to leave one bud on the stub of each lateral. During the third winter, thin laterals from the two main branches to strong shoots about 5 to 11 inches apart. Cut each lateral back to two buds or spurs.

From the fourth winter on, two canes will grow from each spur and bear fruit. During the next dormant season, cut off the cane farthest from the trunk and shorten the cane closest to the trunk to two buds. Each winter repeat this spur pruning so that the remaining canes arch back toward the trunk as they grow.

Grape vines are usually trained to have one or two pairs of arms, but the vine shown here grows in only one direction along the side of a building, where it creates a picturesque setting.

INDEX

Note: Boldface type indicates reference to principal discussion. Italic type indicates illustrations.

U.S. Measure and Metric Measure Conversion Chart

		Formulas for Exact Measures			Rounded Measures for Quick Reference		
	Symbol	When you know:	Multiply by:	To find:			
Mass	oz	ounces	28.35	grams	1 oz		= 30 g
(Weight)	lb	pounds	0.45	kilograms	4 oz		= 115 g
	g	grams	0.035	ounces	8 oz		= 225 g
	kg	kilograms	2.2	pounds	16 oz	= 1 lb	= 450 g
					32 oz	= 2 lb	= 900 g
					36 oz	= 2¼ lb	= 1000g (1 kg)
Volume	pt	pints	0.47	liters	1 c	= 8 oz	= 250 ml
	qt	quarts	0.95	liters	2 c (1 pt)	= 16 oz	= 500 ml
	gal	gallons	3.785	liters	4 c (1 qt)	= 32 oz	= 1 liter
	ml	milliliters	0.034	fluid ounces	4 qt (1 gal)	= 128 oz	= 3¾ liter
Length	in.	inches	2.54	centimeters	⅜ in.		= 1 cm
	ft	feet	30.48	centimeters	1 in.		= 2.5 cm
	yd	yards	0.9144	meters	2 in.		= 5 cm
	mi	miles	1.609	kilometers	2½ in.		= 6.5 cm
	km	kilometers	0.621	miles	12 in. (1 ft)		= 30 cm
	m	meters	1.094	yards	1 yd		= 90 cm
	cm	centimeters	0.39	inches	100 ft		= 30 m
					1 mi		= 1.6 km
Temperature	°F	Fahrenheit	⅝ (after subtracting 32)	Celsius	32°F		= 0°C
	°C	Celsius	⅝ (then add 32)	Fahrenheit	212°F		= 100°C
Area	in.²	square inches	6.452	square centimeters	1 in.²		= 6.5 cm²
	ft²	square feet	929.0	square centimeters	1 ft²		= 930 cm²
	yd²	square yards	8361.0	square centimeters	1 yd²		= 8360 cm²
	a.	acres	0.4047	hectares	1 a.		= 4050 m²